STRATFORD
A Pictorial History

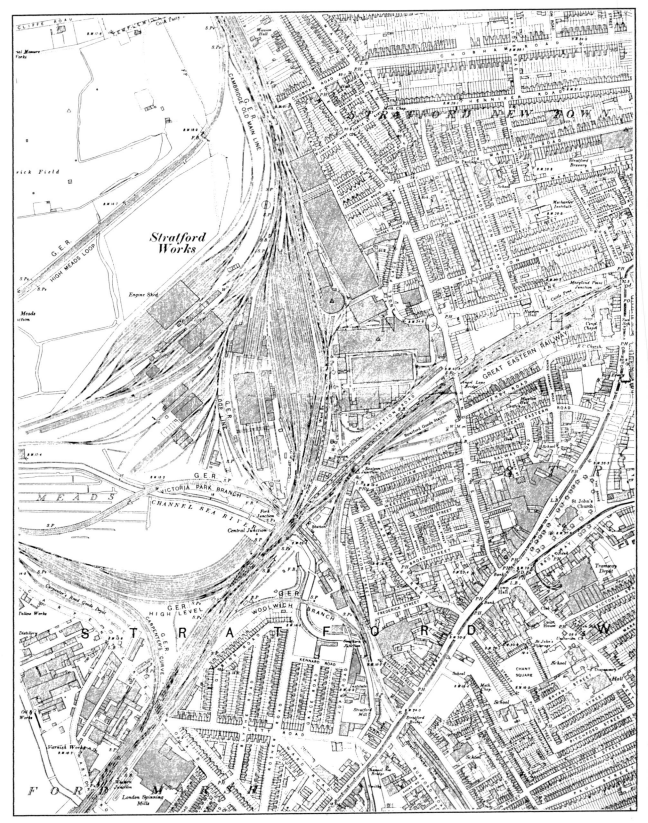

Ordnance Survey Map of 1893

STRATFORD
A Pictorial History

Stephen Pewsey

Phillimore

1993

Published by
PHILLIMORE & CO. LTD.,
Shopwyke Manor Barn, Chichester, West Sussex

ISBN 0 85033 876 X

Printed and bound in Great Britain by
BIDDLES LTD.
Guildford, Surrey

List of Illustrations

Frontispiece: Ordnance Survey Map, 1893

Acknowledgements

Many people have assisted in the creation of this book, and I am most grateful for the generous help I have received. Howard Bloch, Newham Local Studies Librarian, is to be particularly thanked for first enabling me to take up the project, and for his unstinting help during its completion, together with Dorcas Sanders also of the Local Studies Library. Thanks are also due to Bill Storey, for his excellent photography. I would also like to thank Frank Sainsbury, chairman of the Victoria History for the County of Essex for his support and advice, and many helpful suggestions. I am grateful to Newham Libraries Service and Newham Museums Service for permission to reproduce many of the illustrations shown here. Last, but certainly not least, I would like to thank my wife Lynn for her encouragement and infinite patience.

Introduction

Stratford is part of West Ham, one of the ancient parishes of Essex, now within the London Borough of Newham. The boundaries of the ancient parish were determined by local topography: on the west, the Lea and its meandering tributaries; to the south, the Thames; on the north, the Forest of Essex; while to the east lay East Ham, from which West Ham was divided by Ham Creek, once an important waterway but now completely occluded. Extensive tracts of land alongside the Lea and Thames are low-lying and marshy, and this has determined the settlement pattern in the Stratford area.

The name of Stratford, first recorded shortly after the Norman Conquest, indicates its function and importance; it is the Roman road or street which fords the Lea and, as the lowest crossing point of the river for many centuries, it was a situation of some strategic significance. Such places are both boundaries and corridors of communication and, as a focus of road and later rail networks, Stratford is no exception. West Ham was the nearest Essex parish to London, and over the centuries absorbed many influences and settlers from the capital whilst retaining a distinctive identity down to the modern day.

The name Stratford was first applied to the Roman crossing of the Lea, further upstream at Old Ford, and only later to the settlements at both ends of Bow Bridge which spans the Lea. The original Roman crossing—part of the road from London to Colchester—had become dangerous by 1100 and traffic had moved south. The bridge itself was built by Maud, wife of Henry I, shortly after 1100. Traditionally she ordered the bridge to be built after receiving an unceremonious ducking in the Lea as she was crossing there. Maud's arched bridge (hence Bow) was the wonder of its age, and stood the test of time, surviving until 1834. On the Middlesex side lay Stratford-atte-Bow, later simply Bow, while on the Essex side was Stratford Langthorne, named for the abbey, which stood by the road.

Stratford is not separately listed in Domesday Book, but was remarkable for its eight water-mills (there had been nine in 1066), the largest concentration in Essex. The various channels along this stretch of the Lea probably had their origin as mill streams. A small port was built later in the Middle Ages at Stratford for unloading the large quantities of grain brought down the Lea for processing at these mills. According to Domesday Book, the Saxon landowner of West Ham had been one Alestan, but he was replaced after the Conquest by two Normans, Robert Gernon, who held the northern half of the parish, including Stratford, and Ranulph Peverel, who had the southern portion.

Stratford Langthorne Abbey, a Cistercian foundation, was established in 1135 by Robert Gernon's successor William de Montfitchet. The Langthorne, or tall thorn-tree, must have been a prominent and venerable local feature, as it was first mentioned (in a charter) as early as AD 958. The abbey was a wealthy one, due in part to its strategic position close to London. In 1276 Henry III received the papal legate at the abbey, and made peace with the barons there after unsuccessfully trying to revoke some of the freedoms gained in the Magna Carta. Henry's actions caused an insurrection in London, and skeletons with sword cuts found recently during excavations of the Abbey site are thought to relate to this incident.

Henry IV also visited the Abbey in 1411 and 1412. In the Peasants' Revolt of 1381, the abbey was attacked and looted, and its charters were burned.

In the medieval period, the hamlet at Stratford grew slowly as did the other nearby settlements. To the south, the nucleus of West Ham was the parish church, which dates from at least the 12th century, although with many subsequent alterations and additions, whilst at Plaistow, the focus for settlement was around the village green, which occupied the area now bounded by Plaistow High Street, North Street, Pelly Road and Clegg Street. Plaistow means 'place of play', a name first recorded in 1414, and the name is a famous means of identifying outsiders, who always say 'Play-stow' instead of the local (and ancient) pronunciation 'Plar-stow'. Another small settlement was Upton, which as its name implies was on higher ground and inland. Here the 16th-century *Spotted Dog* inn still stands, traditionally associated with Henry VIII. Across the parish boundary, East Ham was a dispersed rural village, with typical Essex 'ends' rather than a single focus; North End, round the present site of East Ham Station, South End at the parish church, and Wall End facing Barking across the Roding.

In the 16th century, Stratford suffered from the religious turbulence affecting the rest of the country; Stratford Langthorne Abbey was dissolved in 1538 and, in the Marian persecutions of 1556, 13 Protestants were burnt at the stake on Stratford Green (probably on the site now occupied by the University of East London campus). A memorial erected to the 'Stratford Martyrs' in 1879 still stands in St John's churchyard in Stratford Broadway. Nonconformity has remained an important component of religious life here, although Catholics have also formed a significant minority.

There was a minor skirmish at Stratford in 1648 during the Civil War. After a number of Royalist risings, one armed band under the Earl of Norwich hoped to march from Greenwich onto London but instead had to flee across the Thames. Their capture by Parliamentarians was bungled and they escaped across Bow Bridge, which was held by Royalists armed with two small cannon. The cavaliers camped at Stratford Green, where they were attacked by Parliamentary forces under Colonel Whalley. The Royalists lost one man but counter-attacked furiously and pushed the roundheads back to Whitechapel, about three men being lost apiece in skirmishes round Bow. They then withdrew back over the bridge and marched first to Romford, and eventually to Colchester which they seized, precipitating the fateful Siege of Colchester.

In the 16th-18th centuries, Stratford was something of a rural retreat for wealthy city merchants, many of whom bought property hereabouts. Examples include Sir Edward Coke (1552-1634), a judge and writer on legal matters, Sir Thomas Foot Bt. (1592-1687), a grocer and former Lord Mayor, Sir Thomas Lodge (?-1584), a former Lord Mayor, Sir Robert Smyth Bt. (?-1699), draper, and Sir John Wittewrong Bt. (?-1693), a brewer of Flemish descent.

At the same time, the Lea valley was becoming more important for industrial activity. Various trades besides flour milling had long been carried on at the various mills in Stratford, including distilling and fulling, and the making of gunpowder. New industries which also sprang up included silk-weaving, important in the 16th and 17th centuries, and calico printing, important from the 17th-19th centuries. The scale of silk-weaving in Stratford can be gauged by the fact that 2,000 people were involved in the Stratford silk riots of 1675, caused by the introduction of mechanical looms. The army were called out to prevent wholesale destruction by the rioters, but many of the new looms were smashed. Calico printing took advantage of the wide meadows beside the Lea to lay out the calico to dry; these were known as the Calico Grounds. The famous Bow porcelain works were also located in Stratford from *c*.1749-*c*.1776 after beginning life on the Middlesex side of the river. Most of the works' finest pieces were produced during the Stratford period, under the direction of local worthy Thomas Frye.

Stratford grew in importance in the 18th and 19th centuries, as a result of its strategic position as London's gateway. The pace of development increased in the first half of the 19th century and growth was phenomenal in the second half. A combination of factors contributed to the growth of Stratford and West Ham.

Initially, there was the arrival of the railways. The Eastern Counties Railway (E.C.R.)—later the Great Eastern—reached Stratford in 1839 and soon pushed on to Brentwood and Colchester. The new Stratford station became a junction as early as 1840, when a line to Broxbourne was opened (eventually extended to Cambridge), and in 1847 a branch line to North Woolwich was added. Further connections were made later, making Stratford a major hub of rail traffic. In 1847 the E.C.R. made Stratford the site of their main works, and locomotive and carriage making remained a major local industry for over a century. A town grew up nearby to house those employed at the works, and was at first known as Hudson Town after the 'Railway King' (and E.C.R. chairman) George Hudson, but changed to Stratford New Town after his fall from grace in a financial scandal.

More or less contemporary with the arrival of the railways was the appearance of the land speculators, in the form of the North Woolwich Land Company. This consortium bought up land fronting the Thames and Lea from 1843 onwards in anticipation of industrial and housing development. This was a most timely move, as in 1844, the Metropolitan Building Act was passed, which regulated various offensive and noxious trades, some of which immediately began looking for a more unfettered working environment, which they found on the Essex side of the Lea and Thames.

Many industries moved to or established themselves in this area over the next 20 or 30 years. The advantages of West Ham were manifold; few regulations, cheap land, an available workforce, and a ready supply of flowing (and relatively pure) water. Land alongside Thames and Lea developed rapidly, with companies such as C. J. Mare & Co., shipbuilders (1846), S. W. Silver & Co., rubber manufacturers (c.1852), and Odams Liquid Manure Works (1855) setting up shop. The latter company used the blood of freshly slaughtered cattle from its own on-site abattoir to produce liquid manure; the stench must have been rather powerful! Other noxious industries attracted to the area were manufacturers of paint, ink, dyes and varnish, fertilisers, soap and pharmaceuticals, and oil refiners.

On the Beckton marshes in East Ham, the largest sewage works and the largest gasworks in the world were both in full production by 1880, adding their own particular odours to those already drifting over the Thames-side area.

Housing, much of it jerry-built, sprang up on low-lying land in the shadow of these various factories and works, at Canning Town, south of West Ham and Plaistow in the 1850s, Silvertown in the same decade. The majority of this housing did not have the benefit of mains water and drainage, and unsurprisingly there were frequent outbreaks of cholera and typhoid.

The greatest industrial venture was, however, the building of the docks, again in the south of the parish. The dock-building programme, promoted by the North Woolwich Land Company, recognised that the existing London docks were too small and badly sited to serve the growing steamship traffic. The Victoria Dock, later the Royal Victoria Dock, was opened in 1855, and encompassed over 80 acres, which at the time was the largest dock in the world. It was equipped with the latest steam haulage and freight handling machinery and was the first dock to be directly connected to the rail network. This was followed by the Royal Albert Dock (partly in East Ham) in 1880, and in 1921, the King George V Dock.

The combination of rapid industrial and population growth put huge pressures on the embryonic local government of the area. St Mary's in Plaistow, built in 1830, and St John's, Stratford, built in 1834, had both become separate ecclesiastical parishes in 1844, but civic administration remained rudimentary. There was a highways board, a poor law board, and the parish vestry, but powers remained ill-defined and roads, sewers and other public utilities that needed attention stayed in the hands of semi-private bodies such as turnpike trusts. The problems of managing a rapidly growing industrial parish came to a head in 1855 when a General Board of Health inquiry headed by Alfred Dickens (the brother of Charles) was severely critical of sanitary conditions in West Ham. As a result, a local board of health was set up the following year and improvements were set in motion. The Metropolitan Board of Works built the Northern Outfall Sewer across West Ham in the 1860s, together with the Abbey Mills Pumping Station, a flamboyant 'Cathedral of Sewage'.

The last half of the 19th century saw unparalleled growth in West Ham. The population practically doubled every decade. In 1851, it was 18,817; in 1861, 38,331; in 1871, 62,919; in 1881, 128,953; and in 1891 it was 204,893. West Ham received municipal borough status in 1886, became a county borough three years later, and was both the largest and the fastest-growing borough in the south of England. The population continued to rise in this century to a peak of no less than 300,860 in 1921, although it then declined steeply to 157,367 shortly before amalgamation with East Ham.

New estates continued to spring up, and Stratford, Plaistow, West Ham and Upton were no longer separated by open country. In Forest Gate, the Gurney and Dames estates were developed from 1855, the Hamfrith and Woodgrange estates from 1877. Upton Manor estate grew up from 1866, and Upton Park in the 1880s. In Stratford, the Carpenters' Company developed the land they held around Carpenters Road from 1867 with a mix of houses and factories. Further south, Custom House was rapidly built up in the 1880s, and by the turn of the century there was very little open land left in the borough.

Stratford Broadway developed as an important shopping centre. J. R. Roberts and Boardman's were two of the best known department stores, and the Co-op also had premises. Founded in 1861 as the Stratford Co-operative Society, after numerous amalgamations it eventually became the London Co-operative Society.

As a result of the population growth, local government worked at a furious pace in the latter years of the 19th century erecting public works: baths, council houses, electricity supply, hospitals, libraries, sewage works and pipes, and tramways. This social intervention was linked to the rise of a strong labour and trade union movement in the area. In 1892, West Ham South returned the first-ever Labour M.P., Keir Hardie, and in 1898 West Ham Council became the first in the country to have a Labour majority. Labour have run the Council from 1919 to the present day without a break, and all West Ham's M.P.s have been Labour since 1934. In the first half of this century, West Ham politics were dominated by Will Thorne (1857-1946), and Jack Jones (1873-1941), both former mayors, longstanding councillors, aldermen, and Members of Parliament for West Ham.

In the First World War under government pressure, the Silvertown works of Brunner Mond & Co. were converted to the production of T.N.T. However the process was highly dangerous, particularly in a densely built-up area, and 69 people died when the works blew up in 1917. In the Second World War, the Blitz affected the borough very badly, particularly in the south around the docks, and by 1945, a quarter of the borough's homes had been destroyed.

Since the war, Stratford has suffered significant industrial decline. The railway works were closed in 1963 and numerous factories have shut down. In the rest of West Ham, the story has been the same. The Royal Docks shut down in the 1980s and there were consequential effects on other Thames-side industries. Stratford town centre underwent radical reshaping in the 1970s with the building of a massive shopping centre and bypass, and the old market in Angel Lane and grandiose Victorian department stores were swept away. The wholesale fruit and vegetable market in Burford Road was closed in 1990. Other markets, which had grown up spontaneously in the last century, also underwent changes; Queens Road market was put under cover in the 1960s, and Rathbone Market was relocated to a windswept site opposite the massive new Canning Town Flyover, the modern counterpart of Queen Maud's arched bridge.

For the future, a revival of Stratford is planned to take the town into the 21st century. Transport has already been modernised with the arrival of the Docklands Light Railway, improving links to East London, and a major interchange for the Channel Tunnel rail link is also planned on the site of the former railway works. Regeneration of the Lea Valley will see the creation of new leisure facilities to link the area into the Lee Valley Park, including museums recalling the milling and pharmaceutical industries that brought Stratford to industrial greatness in the past.

1. West Ham's coat-of-arms was granted in 1886 upon its becoming a municipal borough. The crozier represents Stratford Langthorne Abbey, the ship symbolises the docks, and the hammers stand for the borough's two largest industries (Thames Ironworks and Stratford Railway Works), whilst the chevrons are a variant on the Montfitchet arms; William de Montfitchet founded Stratford Langthorne Abbey.

Early History

As noted in the Introduction, Stratford was an important corn-milling centre from at least as early as the 11th century. The corn came from the surrounding countryside, and Epping Forest, which then stretched almost down to Stratford, provided the enormous quantities of faggots needed to fire the bread ovens. The processing of cattle products also became important in the Middle Ages, at first when Stratford was the final halt for drovers taking cattle into London, then after 1357 when ordinances were issued forbidding the slaughter of cattle any nearer London than Stratford. Butchery then became an increasingly vital Stratford trade, together with the ancillary trades of tanning and leather-working. The plentiful availability of running water, in the Lea and its back rivers, also stimulated the development of various textile trades. Some of the mills were used for fulling, and silk-weaving and calico printing were particularly important, both of which continued into the 19th century.

The presence of Stratford Langthorne Abbey must have brought considerable commerce in both directions through the Abbey gates.

There was (and remains) much confusion over the fact that both settlements on either end of Bow Bridge were at first called Stratford. It is usually stated that the Middlesex settlement was known as Stratford-atte-Bow or Stratford-le-Bow, whilst that on the Essex side was Stratford Langthorne. However, these terms were not always used accurately, and Stratford-le-Bow was sometimes used to describe the built-up area on the causeway between Bow Bridge and Stratford Broadway. This can be seen on Rocque's map below.

The Abbey comprised its own separate parish of St Mary and All Saints; apart from that, Stratford never had its own parochial administration but always formed part of West Ham's parish of All Saints. However, from very early times the parish was divided into several wards, reflecting the dispersed nature of its settlement, so typical of many Essex villages. At first there were four wards; Church Street (i.e. West Ham village), Plaistow, Stratford, and Upton. As Upton later grew less important, it was merged with the Church Street ward.

In the 18th century, as can be seen from both Rocque's map and Chapman and André's map, the four settlements were still separated by fields, and agriculture remained important. The 'villages' remained separate until about 1840, when the pace of development increased. The great Victorian industrial boom was paralleled by an unprecedented surge of house-building, and in particular the southern marshlands were built up; these had previously been used for horse grazing and cattle fattening.

A local board was set up—superseding the old parish government in 1856, which then began to tackle the immense social problems caused by unchecked speculative building. A municipal borough was formed in 1886, and in 1889 a county borough was established, giving it a very large degree of administrative autonomy. Following reorganisation of London government, West Ham was incorporated into Greater London when it was united with the county borough of East Ham in 1965 to form the London Borough of Newham.

EÁDGÁR, 958.

✠ ANNO ab incarnatione domini nostri Ihesu Christi .DCCCC.LVIII. indictione .I. Ego Eadgar, allubescente gratia, rex et primicherius Merciorum, aliquantulam ruris partem, quinis ab accolis aestimatam mansiunculis, in loco qui dicitur Hamme, Æðelstano comiti meo liberam, praeter arcem, pontem, expeditionemque, in perpetuum ius libenter admodum concedo; quatinus diebus uitae suae possideat, et post se cuicunque uoluerit haeredi derelinquat. Quod si quisque, quod non optamus, huiusce donationis cartulam adnichilare temptauerit, coram Christo se rationem redditurum agnoscat. Et his limitibus haec telluris pars circumgyrari uidetur. Ærest of Eádelmes díc on Stocfliót; of ðam flióte tó ilmére; andlang Wynsies mearce on ðone langan þorn; of ðam þornæ on wehincleáge; ðanon on Byrcmære; andlang mære on ðara hina mearcæ; andlang mearce tó Portan beorge; ðanon on Bædewyllan; andlang wylle ðæt innan hile; andlang ealdan hilæ æt ðæra hina mæde; ðanon innan fleót; andlang ðes fleótes on Træfesing múðan; andlang hile on Eádelmes díc. Et huius doni constipulatores exstiterunt quorum inferius nomina carraxari uidentur.

✠ Ego Oscitel episcopus consensi et subscripsi.
✠ Ego Dunstan episcopus consensi et subscripsi.
✠ Ego Cynesige episcopus consensi et subscripsi.
✠ Ego Aðulf episcopus consensi et subscripsi. ✠ Ego Ælfhere dux. ✠ Ego Æðelmund dux. ✠ Ego Æðelwold dux. ✠ Ego Birhtnoð dux. ✠ Ego Æðelsige minister. ✠ Ego Ælfsige minister. ✠ Ego Uffa minister. ✠ Ego Osferð minister. ✠ Ego Winsige minister. ✠ Ego Æðelwold minister. ✠ Ego Byrhtferð minister.

Rubric. Ðis is ðæra landbóc tó Hamme, ðæ Eádgár cing gebócade Æðelstáne bisceope on æce yrfe.

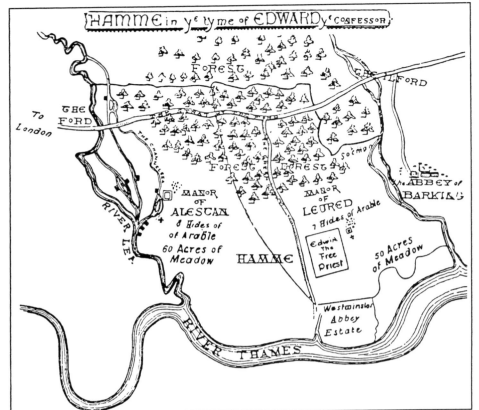

FOREST

GT... ILFORD

To London

THE FORD

Socman

RIVER LEA

FOREST FOREST

ABBEY of BARKING

MANOR OF ALESCAN
8 Hides of of Arable
60 Acres of Meadow

MANOR OF LEURED
7 Hides of Arable

Edwin The Free Priest

50 Acres of Meadow

HAMME

Westminster Abbey Estate

RIVER THAMES

3. The 'Ham' estate at the time of Edward the Confessor; a rather imaginative reconstruction based on an account in Domesday Book. This map first appeared in Katharine Fry's *History of the Parishes of East and West Ham* (1888). A prominent local historian, she was the daughter of the prison reformer Elizabeth Fry.

4. By 1066, as Domesday Book recorded, there was a remarkable concentration of nine water-mills on the Lea and its branches at Stratford. The mills have a complex history, but the earliest recorded by name was known first as Wiggen Mill (probably from the Anglo-Saxon personal name 'Wicga'), and later as Abbey Mill after it was purchased by Stratford Abbey. Shown here in 1832, the Abbey Mills stood on an island in the Channelsea River, and comprised a windmill as well as a water-mill. Rebuilt several times in their long history, Abbey Mills were mainly used for corn milling. Still in use in the 1920s, it was badly damaged in the Second World War and finally demolished in 1967.

5. Bow Bridge, according to legend, originated when Queen Maud (wife of Henry I) received an unexpected ducking in the treacherous crossing of the Lea at Old Ford, about ½ mile north of Stratford. Until then, it had been the main crossing-point of the Lea, but between 1100-18 Queen Maud built Bow Bridge, a marvel of its age because of its wide stone-built single arch, which gave its name, Bow, to a whole neighbourhood. It survived, although much repaired, until 1835 when Queen Maud's Bridge was demolished and replaced in 1839 by a new granite structure, shown in this engraving. In 1905 the bridge had to be replaced and a new and larger iron bridge was opened in 1906. This in turn was overshadowed (literally!) by a huge concrete flyover in 1967 which now carries the bulk of traffic over the Lea.

6. Stratford Langthorne Abbey was founded in 1135 by William de Montfitchet. It was one of the largest Cistercian houses in England, with royal visitors and large land-holdings in West Ham, frequently acting also as an administrative centre for the Becontree Hundred. Its dissolution in 1538 and subsequent demolition was so thorough that no detailed ground plan now exists. A stone window preserved in West Ham church is the only substantial surviving fragment, and recent archaeological work is recovering much information. This engraving shows the Great Gate of the abbey in 1774, which survived until c.1825. A number of other abbey outbuildings also survived as private residences in the 19th century. The Gesten House was put to extraordinary use; it became a home for Lascars, Indian seamen who had settled in this country.

7. A highly imaginative reconstruction of Stratford Langthorne Abbey buildings, drawn in the 1930s.

8. On 27 June 1556, as part of Queen Mary's persecutions, 13 Protestants were burnt at the stake in Stratford. This engraving shows their execution, gruesomely recorded by Foxe in his *Book of Martyrs*. A large crowd of 20,000 turned up 'to watch the burning of Henry Adlington, Thomas Bowyer, Lyon Cawch, John Derifall, Agnes George, William Hallywell, Edmund Hurst, Ralph Jackson, Lawrence Parnam, Elizabeth Pepper, John Routh, George Searles, and Henry Wye'. As can be seen, the eleven men were tied to three stakes, the two women stood loose in the midst. At that time, Stratford Green stretched from the modern reference points of St John's church, Stratford Broadway, to the Passmore Edwards Museum. In 1879, a martyrs' memorial was erected in St John's churchyard, supposedly on the very spot of the executions, although it is now thought more likely that they took place at the eastern end of the Green.

9. In 1599 the 'comedian and buffoon' Will Kemp wagered he would dance all the way from London to Norwich, a feat he achieved in nine days. He later published a tract describing his journey, entitled, *Kemp's Nine Daies Wonder; performed in a daunce from London to Norwich*. He was costumed, as shown in this engraving, in a suit adorned with bells and kerchiefs and accompanied by a 'taberer'. On the first day of his dance he passed through Stratford, where a huge crowd had gathered to see him. Kemp reported that at Stratford a bear-baiting show had been got up in his honour, but so great was the crowd he saw nothing of it, only hearing 'the bear roar and the dogs howl'. This is the only documentary reference to bear-baiting at Stratford.

10. Stratford and district in 1746, as drawn on John Rocque's *Survey of London*. The field boundaries are not very accurate, but the general disposition of the settlement is well represented.

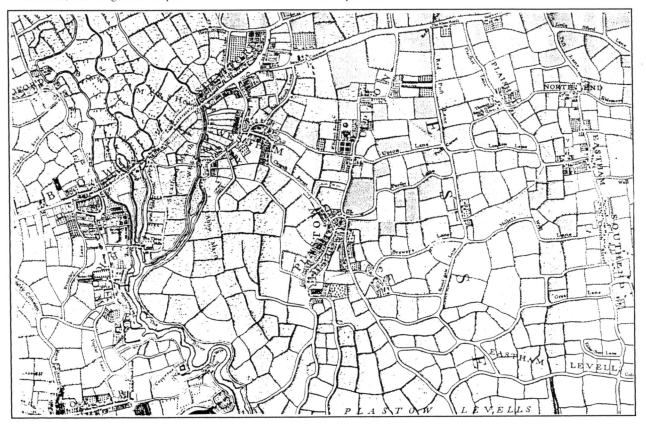

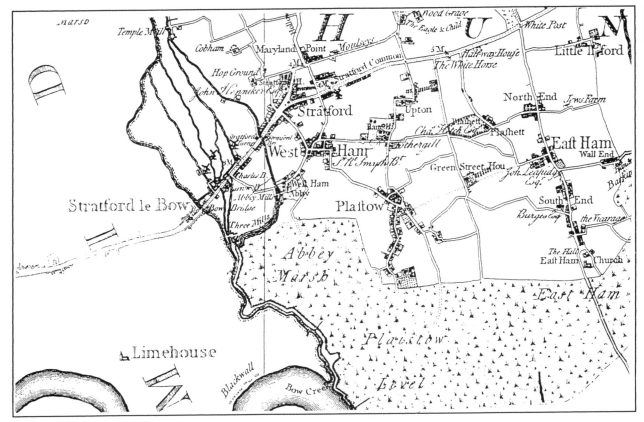

11. Chapman and André mapped the whole of Essex at 2″ to the mile in 1772-4. Their map, published in 1777, was extremely accurate, even depicting many individual buildings. Stratford can be seen as a 'ribbon development' extending along High Street and Broadway from Bow Bridge. John (later Lord) Henniker's residence, Stratford House, is noted, as is Dr. Fothergill's at Ham House, Upton.

12. West Ham as depicted on the 1862 Ordnance Survey map. Considerable growth can be seen around Stratford and Canning Town.

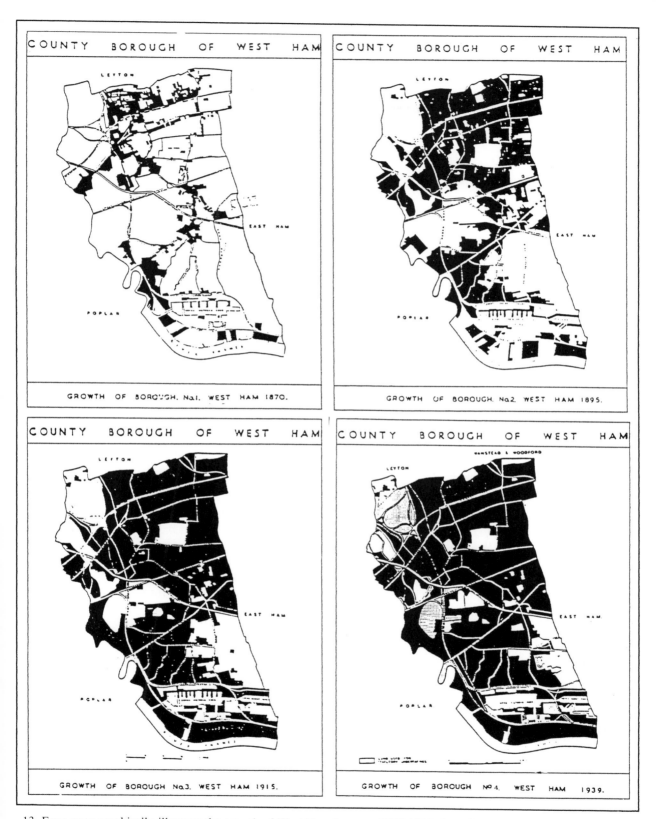

COUNTY BOROUGH OF WEST HAM

GROWTH OF BOROUGH. No.1. WEST HAM 1870.

COUNTY BOROUGH OF WEST HAM

GROWTH OF BOROUGH. No.2. WEST HAM 1895.

COUNTY BOROUGH OF WEST HAM

GROWTH OF BOROUGH No.3. WEST HAM 1915.

COUNTY BOROUGH OF WEST HAM

GROWTH OF BOROUGH No 4. WEST HAM 1939.

13. Four maps graphically illustrate the growth of West Ham between 1870-1939. Over 30,000 houses were built in the borough between 1871-1901, when its population growth made it one of the fastest growing areas in the country.

Stratford Broadway

Stratford Broadway today is an unashamed monument to what former Prime Minister Margaret Thatcher described as 'The Great Car Economy'. Stand outside the *King Edward VII* and watch the endless roar of five or six lanes of traffic, temporarily constrained by the traffic lights, then pelting off westwards towards Bow Bridge. It is the same on Great Eastern Road, north of the Stratford Centre, as the eastbound cars whirl round the gyratory. The heart of Stratford does sometimes seem like a gigantic traffic island. However, was it ever any different? Photographs of Stratford Broadway over the last century and more all reveal the same picture; a mass of moving people on the pavements, a tangle of horse-drawn carriages and carts on the roads, a cobweb of tram-lines, wobbling cyclists and delivery vans, with crossing pedestrians dangerously poised in front of oncoming omnibuses. Stratford is a city of trade, and lives by being a focus for commerce. Broadway is the heart of this trade.

In earlier times, its many inns were the watering-holes that oiled the wheels of industry. The *Swan*, the *King of Prussia* (now *King Edward VII*), *The Bird in Hand*, the *Blue Boar*, and the *Cock* (the latter three all now vanished), plus a dozen other hostelries, were witness to the deals being struck between cattle drovers and butchers, butchers and tanners, corn-factors and mill-owners. A measure of the success of Stratford was the jealousy of city merchants. As early as 1298, the fulling of cloth at Stratford's Lea-side mills provoked protest from city men who felt their monopoly was being threatened. In 1331, city butchers complained that butchers were trading unfairly from Stratford, beyond the city boundaries and thus free of many of the restrictive practices of the city. The bakers of Stratford were also free of these guild restrictions, and thrived. However, the temptations of adulteration and short-weight were sometimes too strong; in 1419 several Stratford bakers were dragged through the City strapped to a hurdle in punishment for just such a transgression.

Stratford grew steadily in the 16th, 17th and 18th centuries; the Broadway was the natural focus for settlement, and buildings crowded along both sides, separated by the wide expanse of Stratford Green, which stretched up to what is now the Stratford campus of the University of East London. In 1722 Daniel Defoe claimed that Stratford had doubled in size in the previous 20 years.

In the 19th century, the arrival of the railway transformed Stratford, which became virtually an entrepôt for London, with goods being brought in by rail for distribution by road and goods brought in by road for rail transhipment. The huge freight and marshalling yards of Stratford station made it a veritable Crewe of the south. Stratford Broadway boomed, its great Victorian emporia, notably Boardman's, Roberts, and the Co-op, tantalising the customer with goods from all over the Empire.

The closure of much of Stratford's industrial base and the growth of out-of-town shopping has led to some diminution of the past commercial glory of Stratford Broadway. However, plans for the regeneration of Stratford through a 'City Challenge' project and its revival as a rail interchange is intended to restore Stratford to its former position as a regional centre.

14. The buildings occupying the site of Stratford Town Hall before it was built. They were described by local historian Dr. Pagenstecher as 'quaint and old-fashioned houses which had to be removed for the new edifice'. A small crowd has gathered in front of the Albion Coffee House to watch a Punch and Judy show.

15. Stratford Town Hall, as depicted in the *Illustrated London News* of 18 September 1869. Giles and Angell designed the building, described in 1908 as a 'handsome structure of stone and brick in the Italian style, ornamented with various figures and groups of statuary, illustrative of the arts and sciences, agriculture, and commerce, and surmounted by a tower, 100 feet in height'. It opened on 7 July 1869.

16. A postcard showing the Town Hall, *c*.1905—always known as Stratford Town Hall, never as West Ham Town Hall. Built in 1867-8, it was enlarged in 1885 to incorporate a court house following the appointment of a stipendiary magistrate. The building of the Town Hall marked significant civic foresight as West Ham did not become a municipal borough until 1886. To the right of the Town Hall, a turntable ladder can be seen; this is standing outside Stratford Fire Station, which was situated next to the Town Hall from 1877-1964. The Town Hall itself was splendidly restored in 1986 after severe fire damage in 1982, and reopened by H.M. the Queen in the year of the municipal centenary.

17. A photograph taken after 1905 showing Stratford Broadway south side, looking towards the Town Hall. A small crowd seems interested by the notice board on the railings of St John's church. They are looking at the 'situations vacant' pages of the *Daily Telegraph*; it was the job of the porter at Stratford Library to take these sheets to the Broadway and paste them on the boards each morning. This was a useful service in times of high unemployment. Tramway Avenue can be seen leading off to the left between the dentist's and the *Swan*; it was built to connect Broadway with West Ham Lane.

18. The north side of Stratford Broadway, *c.*1898.

19. The horse omnibus terminus outside the *Swan*. The *Swan* dates back at least to the early 17th century, and was a coaching halt before it became a bus stop. The present *Swan* dates only from 1925.

20. Cabs for hire, *c*.1895. The cabmen's shelter outside the *Swan* features in a number of photographs of the Broadway.

21. The north side of Stratford Broadway, *c.*1895; a splendid array of emporia.

22. Market stalls in the Broadway, Saturday, 2 May 1925 at 2.30 p.m. Stall-holders had been trading in the Broadway since at least 1858, but were not officially licensed until 1925. This photograph is part of the official archive of the first day's legitimate trading.

23. The *King of Prussia* in Stratford Broadway dates back to at least 1765, and was probably named after Frederick the Great (King 1740-86). Rebuilt early in the 19th century, the name was quickly changed at the outbreak of the First World War to the *King Edward VII*.

Churches

The parish church of All Saints West Ham, about ½km south of Stratford town centre, is the oldest surviving building in the area. It dates back at least to the 12th century, with some earlier references to a priest indicating the possibility of an earlier church. As it now stands, the building is a story in stone; additions and accretions have all but obscured the earliest church, which at one time had transepts giving it a regular cruciform shape. Essentially built of ragstone and flint-rubble, later additions have mainly been in brick, and the fine tower—which must once have been a prominent landmark—is constructed from Reigate stone. Little but the clerestory remains from the 12th century. The two aisles were added at an unknown date, although the arcades date from around 1240. The tower was added about 1400. The south chapel is 15th century, the north chapel, of red brick, was added c.1550. The interior is adorned with a number of fine monuments which hark back to the days when West Ham was a rural retreat for city merchants such as James Wittewrong and Sir Thomas Foot, Bt.

The rapid expansion in population necessitated the creation of many new parishes and a large-scale building programme, some of which are illustrated below. In 1903, the Church of England had no less than 41 churches in West Ham, including mission churches. However, while Anglicanism was the largest single denomination in West Ham, the protestant nonconformist churches had a far larger collective congregation. In 1903, Anglican attendance in West Ham was recorded as 17,643 at all its churches. Nonconformist churches however had a combined attendance of 31,414, the largest single denomination being the Congregational church, with 7,318. The various strands of Methodism, however between them had over 9,000 attending. Nonconformism was a powerful force in West Ham politics and social life, and was closely tied up with socialist politics and agitation for improved social conditions. The principles of campaigning, socially-reforming Christianity in West Ham went back at least to the 18th century when many leading Quakers lived in the area.

Roman Catholicism has also played a considerable part in the life of West Ham. Once again, referring to the 1903 survey, there were 6,592 Catholics attending mass, more than any other place in Essex or the outer metropolis. Stratford was the first Roman Catholic parish in Essex to be formed after Catholic emancipation. The presence of large numbers of Irish agricultural workers in West Ham helped to swell the numbers of communicants, but churches such as St Antony of Padua in Forest Gate also attracted middle-class worshippers from parts of London and elsewhere in Essex.

Many churches were destroyed or damaged in the Blitz and, together with declining attendances, the churches were experiencing difficulty by 1939. The post-war period has, therefore, seen a great deal of rationalisation and reorganisation of parishes and buildings. Many churches have been rebuilt on a smaller scale, whilst others have disappeared altogether or lie derelict awaiting conversion which, unfortunately, leaves them to the mercy of vandals.

24. West Ham church at the turn of the century. The parish church of All Saints is the oldest surviving building in West Ham, and the settlement of Church Street (as the ward around West Ham church was earlier known) radiates outwards. The church is basically 12th century, but has undergone a great many alterations and extensions in its long history, including the addition of aisles in the 13th century, and the tower in the 15th century. There may have been a church earlier than the 12th century as a priest named Ranulph owned land in West Ham before 1135. The name of West Ham as a separate area does not occur until the middle of the 12th century.

25. A rather idealised engraving of West Ham parish church and village in 1832.

26. St John's church, Stratford Broadway, 1925. The church was built in 1834, at first as a chapel of ease, then with its own parish after 1844. The site had originally been part of the village green, and once contained the lock-up as well as a blacksmith's and a cow-house. In the foreground stands the Gurney Memorial, erected for philanthropist Samuel Gurney in 1861.

27. St Mary's church, Plaistow, was the second church to be built in the parish of West Ham, after All Saints itself. Erected in 1830 as a chapel of ease, it became a parish church in its own right in 1844. Two incumbents saw Plaistow transformed from an agricultural village into a bustling suburb; these were R. W. B. Marsh (vicar 1842-84), and Thomas Given-Wilson (vicar 1884-1914). Given-Wilson adopted an energetic policy of parish assistance to the poorer residents, sending pamphlets around the world appealing for aid. Through his philanthropic work, and the large donations received, two convalescent homes were built in Southend-on-Sea, and the former St Mary's Hospital for Women and Children was largely his foundation, and he organised medical care for the poor. The engraving shows the first St Mary's; it was rebuilt on a grand scale by Given-Wilson in 1894, and again in 1981 on a much smaller scale.

28. An unusual drawing from the 1930s of the spire of Holy Trinity church, Barking Road, seen from across the roof-tops of Canning Town. The church was a massive Victorian pile erected in 1867 to evangelise the then rapidly-growing districts of Hallsville and Canning Town. Damaged in the Blitz, the church was closed in 1948 and demolished in 1961.

29. Emmanuel Church Forest Gate, Romford Road, was part of the huge increase in church building to cope with the rapidly growing population at Stratford and West Ham in the latter part of the 19th century. Emmanuel was built in 1852 and a parish carved out of the ancient parishes of East and West Ham in 1853. Designed by Sir Gilbert Scott, it was enlarged several times and still stands today.

Congregational Church & Schools. North St.

30. The Congregational church, Plaistow, built in 1807. In 1860, the church moved to Balaam Street under its famous minister John Curwen, who invented the tonic sol-fa system of musical notation. After the church moved, the buildings then became part of the Curwen Press. Beside the church stands the schoolroom, opened in 1844 under the conscientious master Alfred Brown, who remained in a position of authority until his death in 1886, despite the school's transfer to the West Ham Board in 1872.

31. Stratford Congregational church, The Grove, was one of the largest nonconformist churches in Stratford. Built in 1866-7, its design was so grandiose it was known as 'Settles' Folly' after the wealthy city merchant William Settles who was the driving force behind its construction. The church, pictured here c.1900, could seat 1,600 and was for some time a stronghold of Liberal politics in West Ham. It was closed in 1948, becoming a furniture factory. After being damaged by fire in 1950, it was demolished in 1952.

32. Pelly Road Methodist church, Plaistow, in 1903. It was built in 1870-1 and stood on the corner of Grafton Road; the church was sold in 1903 to the Congregationalists. Methodism was a strong influence on local life in East and West Ham and many prominent politicians were also leading Methodists. John Wesley himself had visited Plaistow in September 1739 and, as a result of other visits to Stratford, a chapel was founded in the High Street by 1790.

33. The Friends' Meeting House, Plaistow. Quakers were active in West Ham from the middle of the 17th century, and a meeting house was built in North Street, Plaistow, in 1704. A larger house, shown here, was built in 1823. This became a board school in 1872 and survived, much altered, until 1969. Quakerism was a vigorous social force in West Ham, and many of the leading local families were Quakers; the Gurneys and Barclays (both banking families), the Listers (Lord Lister, the pioneer of antiseptic surgery), and the Howards (Luke Howard, chemist and pharmaceutical manufacturer). Influential visitors to the house included William Wilberforce, John Wesley and John Bright.

34. Despite the fact that there were 137 churches in West Ham in 1903, only about a fifth of the population attended church. This led various evangelistic organisations to take to the streets to give bible-readings and services on street corners. The Salvation Army was of course the most forthright in this crusade, but a number of itinerant preachers worked unsung and alone in the most deprived areas. In this photograph, a travelling minister gives a bible-reading to coalmen working at E. A. Shadrack's coalyards in the Barking Road. Shadrack's was one of West Ham's biggest coal merchants.

Public Buildings and Utilities

Sewage and its disposal were for a long time the overriding obsession of the good burgesses of Stratford. Indeed, it may be said that the modern system of local government in Britain was largely created out of a need to rationalise the disposal of human waste. The connection between inadequate drainage and epidemics of infectious diseases, such as cholera and typhoid, was at last being made in the mid-Victorian period, just at the time when overcrowded suburbs were perfect breeding grounds for such plagues. However, in Stratford and West Ham, the problem of jerry-built and insanitary dwellings, without proper supply of potable water or provision for waste disposal, lasted well into this century.

The chief difficulty was undoubtedly the sheer speed of growth. Between 1801 and 1851, the parish of West Ham grew in population from 6,485 to 18,817. Every decade after that it doubled, or virtually doubled, in size until by 1921 it had reached an incredible peak of 300,860 and was easily the most populous district in southern England.

In the early years of the 19th century, West Ham's parish administration had changed little since the Middle Ages. However, by the 1850s, rows of squalid terraces were springing up in Canning Town and on Plaistow Marshes, in the wake of the building of the Victoria Dock and the arrival of new industries. These speculative developments were not provided with mains water, sewage disposal, or even roads and, not surprisingly, living conditions were dire. In 1855 a report by the government's General Board of Health, written by Alfred Dickens (Charles' brother) about sanitary conditions in West Ham was unsparing in its criticism:

> The whole parish is divided and subdivided by open ditches and sewers, and in no instance ... did I find one that was not horribly filthy and offensive. They are usually stagnant and filled with refuse of the foulest description; their smell being sickening in the extreme. It was impossible to describe the miserable state Canning Town was in; there was neither drainage nor paving; in winter the streets were impassable; the cholera raged very much in this district. Many houses under water after rain. This district is completely unpaved, the roads are not dedicated to the parish, and they remain with last winter's ruts, in some cases two or three feet deep; although the roads are left in this state the inhabitants pay a highway rate for the rest of the parish. Deep holes at intervals in the middle of the streets filled with stagnant water, pigs wallowing in some of these filthy spots.

Following this graphic description, there was a recommendation for a Local Board of Health to be established to tackle the problems, and this was duly elected in 1856. The board completely revised the system of sewerage and drainage, and also oversaw the paving of some streets. They also prepared the way for the creation of the municipal council by the building of Stratford Town Hall. However, the problem of sewage disposal was not fully resolved until 1901, when West Ham was finally connected to the Northern Outfall Sewer.

Gas lighting came to West Ham in the 1850s, supplied by the West Ham Gas Co. The Gas Light and Coke Company, with its giant gasworks nearby in Beckton, came to dominate gas supply in the area until post-war nationalisation.

Electricity was from the start a corporation concern, and electrification was undoubtedly seen as a key component in the effort to modernise the borough. It was promoted vigorously by the corporation and was a highly efficient undertaking. Nationalisation came in 1947.

35. West Ham had hand fire-pumps as early as 1792, but the service was extensively modernised in 1877 when new tenders and stations were provided at Stratford and Canning Town. Motorised fire escapes began service as early as 1909, but magnificent horse-drawn engines, such as the one shown here c.1870, remained in service until 1923.

36. This is Stratford's most important group of surviving Victorian public buildings. On the left and in the centre of the picture are the Central Library and the Technical Institute respectively, both buildings being opened in 1898. In 1921 the Technical Institute became West Ham Municipal College, more recently a polytechnic and in 1992 renamed the University of East London. On the right is the shallow dome over the banded brick of the Passmore Edwards Museum, opened in 1900. The buildings were designed by J. G. S. Gibson and S. B. Russell in red brick with elaborate stone friezes and facings. It was paid for by a share given to West Ham of customs duties paid at the Port of London, the so-called 'whisky money'. The buildings stand on the site of Stratford Green, also known as Gallows Green, where 13 Protestants were burnt at the stake in 1556 (*see* illustration 8).

37. Canning Town Public Hall was opened in 1894. Designed by Lewis Angell it provided a focus for civic administration in the south of the borough; Stratford was hard to reach from Canning Town and the Docklands. As it stood on the site of a well-known local 'speakers' corner'—Will Thorne's gas workers union had been founded here—Canning Town Public Hall continued to act as the focus for socialist and trades union agitation. In 1893 the philanthropist Passmore Edwards opened Canning Town Public Library (seen next door with turret), with 1,000 books of the initial stock paid for by Passmore Edwards.

38. The Passmore Edwards Museum (earlier known as the Essex Museum), Romford Road, Stratford. The museum was opened on 18 October 1900 by the Countess of Warwick and houses the collections of the Essex Field Club. It was originally intended to form the final link in a trio of county museums covering the history and natural history of Essex: the other two are at Colchester and Chelmsford, and retain the county name in their title. The Essex Field Club, formed in 1880, is still based at the museum and promotes interest in both natural history and archaeology. Comprehensively refurbished in 1990, the museum is also the headquarters of a most valuable archaeological service which undertakes excavations throughout Metropolitan and south-west Essex.

39. Stratford's first public library was opened in Rokeby House, Stratford Broadway, in 1892. Stratford Central Library, Water Lane, was opened in October 1898. Part of the museum and college complex, it has provided a focus and launch-pad for some of the boroughs many clubs and societies.

40. West Ham obtained powers to generate electricity as early as 1892, and provided electric lighting to Canning Town Public Hall and Library by 1896. In 1899 the splendidly-named 'Tramways and Electric Lighting Committee' was formed to direct policy on electrification within the borough. Canning Town Generating Station opened in April 1904 in Quadrant Street. This photograph shows the station shortly after opening.

41. An interior view of Canning Town Generating Station, the capacity of which was expanded enormously during its lifetime to cope with the demands of industrial and domestic electrification.

42. This photograph, taken *c*.1930, shows electric vehicles belonging to the West Ham electricity undertaking, with their smartly uniformed service engineers alongside. The headquarters of the utility were at 84 Romford Road, first opened in 1906 and rebuilt on a vast scale in 1927-30.

43. Mid-Victorian London's booming population overloaded the medieval sewage system. The Metropolitan Board of Works was formed in order to re-organise the capital's waste disposal arrangements. The brilliant—but sadly unsung—civil engineer Joseph Bazalgette designed an elegantly simple solution. A large outfall sewer was to be built on either side of the Thames fed by a grid of inner-city sewers. The outfall sewers ran out of the capital and discharged the effluent beyond the range of London nostrils. Pumping stations en route ensured a steady rate of flow. The finest of these was built at Abbey Mills, Stratford, and opened in 1868. This architecturally spectacular 'Cathedral of Sewage' was originally powered by four vast beam engines. The pumping station is still in use today, a monument to the high age of Victorian civil engineering. The two tall flanking chimneys were removed at the outbreak of the Second World War.

On the sign in the image:

> June 16th
> Dongola Rd
> all from
> Balaam St

> 380 Tubes
> 330 Complete
> 600 Open Cut

44. Barking Road Relief Sewer being laid in Dongola Road. West Ham had always had difficulty with the disposal of sewage. Much of the jerry-built property on the marshes in the south of the borough had only open ditches for both drinking water and sewage disposal. When the West Ham Local Board was formed in 1856 its first task was to sort out the problem. Unfortunately the Metropolitan Board of Works did not permit the West Ham authorities to connect West Ham's sewers to the Northern Outfall Sewer, so separate outfall works had to be constructed, at great cost, at Bow Creek and Silvertown. This unsatisfactory arrangement continued until 1901, when local sewers were finally connected to the Northern Outfall.

45. West Marsh Sewer, Manor Road. One of the many open ditches which drained the marshes in the southern part of the borough; the low-lying land has a miserably bleak aspect.

46. Concern over the hygiene of the booming population of Stratford led one William Hawes to give a lecture there in 1853 entitled 'Baths and Wash Houses for the Industrious Classes'. However, nothing came of this, and it was not until the early years of the 20th century that public slipper baths began to be provided by the municipal authorities. The area, however, remained one of the worst for provision of indoor bathrooms in the country. West Ham Baths, with associated slipper baths, opened in Romford Road in 1934; this advertisement dates from 1955.

Shops and Streets

Mention has already been made of the great department stores of Stratford Broadway. The illustrations below are intended to convey something of the vibrancy of everyday shopping in Stratford and West Ham, something recalled by all older residents. The banter, the bargaining, the street-corner huckster, the patter of the market stall-holder, the personal service and courtesy, all loom strongly in the memory. The markets had a distinctive smell; the toffee-apple man, the bloater-and-kipper man, the roast-peanut man. As well as West Ham's three retail markets (Stratford, Rathbone Street and Queen's Road), there was also a wholesale fruit and vegetable market, opened off Stratford High Street in 1879. Directly served by rail, it was a considerable rival to the East End's Spitalfield's market in its heyday. It was closed in advance of the extension of the Jubilee Line to Stratford at the end of the 1980s.

47. North Woolwich Road looking east from Tidal Basin swingbridge, *c.*1884. This busy road served the industries of Silvertown, flanked by the Silvertown Tramway. The Tramway began life as the North Woolwich branch of the Eastern Counties Railway in 1847, but the line was re-routed north of the Royal Victoria Dock when the dock was built. The tramway then served as a shuttle for areas south of the dock, and its swingbridge over Tidal Basin was a well-known traffic bottleneck. Behind the *Ram Tavern* and Victoria Coffee and Dining Rooms, on the right of the picture, stood the great industrial concerns of Silvertown, extending down to the Thames.

Street scenes, like shops, are a social barometer. They convey the exact flavour of the period, and the following photographs have been selected on the basis both of a good geographical coverage of all parts of the borough, together with a good dollop of 'reminiscence quota'. Stratford was bustling and so was Victoria Dock Road, but the bustle was of a different order, and, as in any locality, there were minute social differences associated with living in one particular street as opposed to another, or attending a particular church or doctor, just as there are today. This is one of the most fascinating aspects of social history. Nothing can be more melancholic than the photograph of a deserted Angel Lane, where Harold and Laura Pewsey, my grandfather and grandmother, lived with their young family for a time in the 1930s. Angel Lane, with its frenetic street-market trading till all hours, must have been one of the busiest, liveliest roads in Metropolitan Essex, and a visit to Angel Lane was always nearly as good as a trip 'up West', to London itself. Nevertheless, the shuttered shops and torn advertisements, the stillness of a Sunday perhaps, also form part of the picture of Stratford's history.

48. Victoria Dock Road in 1884. Beyond Simpson's the builders stands Relf's Music Hall, opened in 1875. Rebuilt several times, it was later known as the Royal Albert, then as the New Imperial, before being converted to a cinema. It was demolished in 1967 after a spell as a bingo club.

49. An 1898 advertisement for J. R. Roberts, one of the great department stores of Stratford. (Sir) J. R. Roberts was a distinguished 'merchant prince' of Stratford who had considerable influence in the area.

50. Star Lane, Canning Town, *c.*1890 was a typical late 19th-century terrace. It was originally a country lane so-named because it led to a Star Field, but was built up when Canning Town rapidly developed after the 1880s.

51. Beckton Road in 1890. This area of Canning Town contained many jerry-built houses and its squalour was criticised in Alfred Dickens' 1855 report on sanitary conditions in the area.

52. An advertisement for Boardman's dating from 1896. Boardman's, Roberts' and the Co-op were the three major stores of Stratford.

53. The Freemasons Road Dispensary (now demolished) was situated at Aberdeen House, Canning Town. 'Midwifery, vaccination, teeth extracted' were advertised when this photograph was taken on 20 October 1891. By and large, medical provision in Canning Town and the docklands was very inadequate at this time.

54. Stratford pioneered the co-operative movement. Railway workers formed the Stratford Co-operative and Industrial Society in 1861 and opened a shop in Stratford New Town (north of Stratford Broadway) the following year. The shop expanded enormously in the following years and became one of the leading stores of Stratford. Amalgamating with the Edmonton Society in 1920, the Stratford Society became the London Co-operative Society. There is still a Co-op store in Stratford Broadway.

55. Victoria Dock Road level crossing, known locally as 'The White Gates', *c.*1903. This was a notorious traffic bottleneck. Behind, the *Black Prince* nears completion in the Thames Ironworks. The vessel was launched in 1904, one of the last big naval ships to be built at the 'Thames'.

56. Maryland Point lies between Stratford and Leytonstone, around Maryland Station. This curious name first appeared on a map of 1696, when it was shown as a new district of Stratford. It was probably given that name by one Richard Lee, a wealthy merchant who emigrated to Virginia, *c*.1640. There he owned an estate in Maryland on the Potomac River. When he returned to England in 1658, he bought land at Stratford and named his estate Maryland Point. This photograph dates from the early years of the 20th century when Maryland was a prosperous shopping centre. The Trinity Presbyterian church was a prominent landmark. Built in 1879, it was closed in 1941, then used as a furniture factory until it burnt down in 1953.

57. Kingsland Road, Plaistow, typifies much of the better class of artisans' dwellings erected throughout the borough in the late Victorian and Edwardian periods. This long street of terraced houses was completed in 1904, part of the Bemersyde estate built up from 1870 by developer Henry Haig (1818-97). Haig was a distant relative of the noble Haig family of Bemersyde, Roxburghshire, hence the name. No road traffic in those days, except the hand-cart!

58. Dock Road and Tidal Basin Road junction, looking west from the level crossing. This busy scene was photographed in April 1904.

59. Woodgrange Road in 1902. It was and remains an important shopping thoroughfare, particularly for Forest Gate residents. Spratt's drapers stands on the right, and the spires of the Wesleyan Methodist church lie beyond. Built in 1881-82, this church had the largest Protestant congregation in the borough by 1903, and still had a congregation of 800 by 1939. Bombed in the war, the church was rebuilt in 1962. Forest Gate Station stands at the far end of the road; opened by 1841, it was the original terminus of the London Tilbury & Southend Railway.

60. The Grove, Stratford, *c*.1901. This road leading north from Stratford Broadway was once lined with a number of substantial private residences, including Stratford House, the seat of the Henniker family who were important local landowners. The poet Gerard Manley Hopkins was born at No. 87 The Grove in 1844. As the area became less attractive, the residences were converted into offices or demolished.

61. Stone's: a typical Canning Town grocer, *c*.1900. Occupying No. 231 Hermit Road, the shop had an unusual narrow corner position; the bright and bold window display made the best of the location. The advertisements are a fascinating social documentary in their own right; Borwick's baking powder, Bird's custard, Ovum poultry products, Spratt's dog biscuits and six grades of flour sold by the quartern (a quarter of a stone or 3½ pounds).

62. 73-75 Upton Lane, July 1902. Note the prominent advertisements for Jeyes' Fluid; John Jeyes established Jeyes Sanitary Compounds Co. in Plaistow in 1885 to market the first commercially available germicide, which he had patented.

63. Hard to believe from this quiet scene, but Angel Lane was one of the busiest and most important shopping thoroughfares in Metropolitan Essex, attracting shoppers from all over East London and south-west Essex. Older residents nostalgically recall the bustling late-night market lit by naphtha flares; visiting the market was often a family occasion enlivened by the cutting wit of the traders.

64. Pelly Road, Plaistow, *c.*1902, looking south to the railway bridge. Latham's store is situated on the corner of Terrace Road and Pelly Road, whilst the Methodist church stands opposite.

65. Green Street in 1904 was, and still is, a thriving shopping thoroughfare. There is still a branch of Boots on the corner of Harold Road. The borough boundary lay down the middle of Green Street, with West Ham to the left and East Ham to the right. Once known as Gipsy Lane, the area is now characterised by bustling enterprises run by Asian and Asian-descent shopkeepers. The cosmopolitan atmosphere attracts shoppers from as far afield as Nottingham and Leicester.

66. Stratford High Street, c.1904. Although it was originally the focus for shops and trading, as this dismal scene indicates, businesses gradually moved east to Broadway and Angel Lane; High Street was then given over to industrial concerns.

67. Romford Road, Forest Gate, c.1902, showing West Ham brewery. Despite its grandiose billboard, the brewery was a short-lived enterprise. Stratford was better known for distilling rather than brewing, thanks to the large number of mills.

68. West Ham Lane in 1902 was a charming scene. The road ran between Stratford Broadway and West Ham parish church, and despite Edwardian development in the area many of the ancient buildings remained. Unfortunately this is not the case today.

69. Turpin's, Barking Road, in 1909. This stolid yellow-brick store was West Ham's largest linoleum and carpet shop, first established in 1895, and still in existence today. The Turpin family have sometimes claimed descent from the highwayman Dick Turpin (1705-39), who by local tradition worked for a time as a farmer's hand in Plaistow and married an East Ham girl.

70. Nos. 61-77 Upton Lane, at the junction with Studley Road, featuring some fascinating window and street displays by the Edwardian shopkeepers. This is still a street of small shops and, aside from the traffic, the scene today is much the same as it was a century ago!

71. Henry 'Mackio' Larkin and his wife Liz (centre) at their shop, No.39 Freemasons Road, *c*.1910. The Larkins were a very large and well-known Canning Town family with a number of shops and stalls in East and West Ham, and were famous for their ice cream. 'Mackio' himself was best known as 'The Peanut King'; in 1897 he invented a method of mechanically roasting peanuts, which he sold in little paper bags bearing his slogan 'The Peanut King'.

72. Queens Road market originated about 1903 when street traders were moved out of Green Street by West Ham council. It was well established by 1911 and thrived between the wars. In the late 1960s the open-air market was closed down and replaced with a large concrete roofed concourse providing trading under cover for stall-holders.

73. Rathbone market, *c.*1925; is the borough's last open air market. It originated in the 1880s in Victoria Dock Road, which was then privately owned by the Dock company. However, although the council obtained some statutory powers over the street traders, it was the increase in traffic which forced the stall-holders to move into nearby Rathbone Street, where this photograph was taken. There was a further move in 1963 to the present site in Barking Road, in connection with the general redevelopment of the area and the construction of the new Canning Town flyover.

LOT 5.

ALL THAT SUBSTANTIALLY-BUILT

Long Leasehold Corner Shop and Adjoining House

situate and being

Nos. 229 & 231, STAR LANE, Barking Road, Plaistow.

The accommodation afforded is as follows :—

As to No. 229.

On the FIRST FLOOR—Front and back bedrooms each fitted with stove.

On the GROUND FLOOR—Front room fitted with stove ; Kitchen with range, dresser and cupboard ; Scullery with copper, sink and water supply ; W.C. and yard at rear.

As to No. 231.   In the occupation of a grocer and provision dealer.

On the SECOND FLOOR—Front and back bedrooms each fitted with stove.

On the FIRST FLOOR—Front sitting room fitted with stove ; Back bedroom ; Off room with range and water supply.   On the GROUND FLOOR—**Double-fronted Shop ;** Back room ; Scullery with copper, sink and water supply ; Private entrance door ; W.C. and yard at rear with gateway entrance.

They are let as follows :—

No.	Standard rent.	Increase of rent.	Excess rates.	Total per week.	Total per annum.
229	7/6	2/1	2/3	11/10	£30 15 4
231	14/-	4/1	4/5	22/6	£58 10 0

Total amount paid per annum   <u>£89 5 4</u>

landlord paying outgoings.

Held upon lease for a term of 99 years from the 29th September, 1882 (leaving 55½ years unexpired) at the low ground rent of £7 5s. 0d. per ann

LOT 6.   ALL THOSE

Four Well=Built Long Leasehold Dwelling Houses

situate and being

Nos. 93, 95, 97 & 99, DONGOLA ROAD, Barking Road, Plaistow.

Situate a few yards from the main road and a short distance from the Greengate Public House.

The houses have enclosed forecourts and bay windows to the ground floor front rooms.

They each contain :—

On the FIRST FLOOR—Front room with stove ; Back room fitted with stove ; Half landing, Back room.

On the GROUND FLOOR—Front parlour fitted with stove ; Back room fitted with stove ; Kitchen with range and dresser ; Scullery with copper, sink and water supply. W.C. and garden at rear.

They are let as follows :—

No.	Standard rent.	Increase of rent.	Excess rates.	Total per week.	Total per annum.
93	9/6	2/8	3/-	15/2	£39 8 8
95	9/6	2/8	3/-	15/2	£39 8 8
97	9/6	2/8	3/-	15/2	£39 8 8
99	(partly decontrolled) now paying 17/- per week				£44 4 0

Total amount paid per annum   <u>£162 10 0</u>

landlord paying outgoings.

Held upon lease for a term of 99 years from the 25th December, 1884 (leaving 57¾ years unexpired) at the low ground rent of £13 10s. 0d. per ann. for the four houses.

74. Part of a fascinating 1926 sales catalogue for properties mainly in Plaistow, giving interesting details of house interiors and rents of terraced dwellings.

75. Barking Road, 22 August 1930. In the distance on the right, the roof of the Grand Cinema can be seen. Opened in 1913, it did not survive the Blitz. Barking Road was built in 1812 by the Commercial Road Turnpike Trust to link the India Docks and Barking. Its long stretch of shops later made it a natural commercial focus for the southern parts of West Ham.

76. Ridley's grocery shop, Cullum Street, Stratford, c.1930. A typical scene, with the ever-present posse of small boys. This shop was reputedly the first property in West Ham to purchase an electric stove, some time between 1926 and 1930. Cullum Street, which ran off Angel Lane, was demolished as part of the 1960s redevelopment of Stratford.

77. A glorious display of fruit and vegetables at Rees & Sons in Barking Road. The shop lay between Prince Regent Lane and Tunmarsh Lane. The photograph was taken on 10 October 1930.

78. Plans illustrating proposals for resolving the long-standing traffic problems in the Royal Docks area. Improvement schemes were first put forward as early as 1915, but it was 1933-4 before the Silvertown Way and Silvertown bypass, both viaducts, were built, giving a clear through route for the first time.

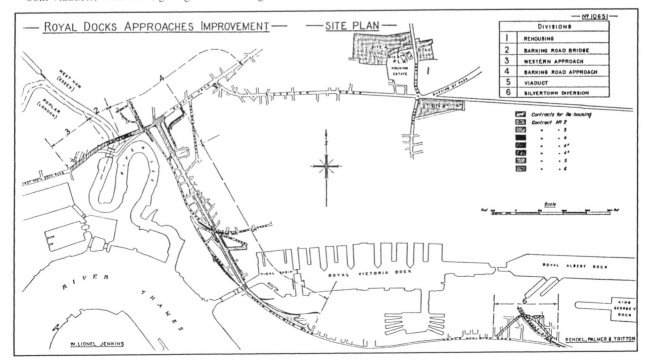

79. Silvertown Way under construction, 29 September 1933. It was opened in 1934 and the viaduct did away with the bottleneck associated with the swing bridge at Tidal Basin, although many families were displaced when houses in the path of the viaduct had to be demolished. A new estate was constructed for them in Prince Regent Lane.

80. Almshouses in Church Passage, West Ham, 1940. Built in 1745-8 as a result of the £200 bequest by James Cooper, they were demolished in February 1944 following the building of new almshouses in Gift Lane. The almshouses provided accommodation for 20 poor women.

81. The concrete flyover at Bow, shortly after opening in 1967. This new flyover eclipsed the 1905 iron bridge beneath.

Public Houses

As a market town and coaching stop, Stratford had a considerable number of inns and public houses, some of which survive, though rebuilt in the 19th and 20th centuries. Ogilby's *Traveller's Guide* of 1674 described Stratford as 'chiefly consisting of inns'. The outlying hamlets (as they then were) of West Ham and Plaistow also had their fair share of inns, and by 1740 there were more than 60 public houses in the parish. This seems to have been a peak, as the numbers slowly fell back from then on, down to 46 in 1749, 34 in 1795, and

32 in 1815. Beer was at that time regarded more as an essential commodity along with bread and salt than as a social habit.

Some of the public houses were of considerable antiquity, such as the *Abbey Arms*, *Black Lion*, *Coach & Horses*, and *Greyhound*, all in Plaistow, while Upton's *Spotted Dog* is the oldest building (excluding the ancient parish churches) in the whole of East and West Ham. In Stratford Broadway some old pubs have disappeared; the *Angel*, the *Cart and Horses* and the *Yorkshire Grey*, but the *King Edward VII* (earlier *King of Prussia*), and the *Swan* are over 200 years old, as is the *Pigeons* in Romford Road nearby.

With the growth of population, large numbers of drinking-houses sprang up in the south of the borough. Victoria Dock Road in particular was well supplied with pubs, and some establishments such as the *Connaught Tavern* were placed right outside the dock gates, no doubt to the delight of thirsty dockers and visiting seamen.

The oddly-named *Adam and Eve*, off Abbey Road, stands on the site of the church of Stratford Langthorne Abbey, and was reported in the 18th century to be 'a rendez-vous for fellows and wenches in the summer'!

82. The *Old Spotted Dog*, Upton Lane, is the borough's oldest secular building. It is a timber-framed hall of the 16th century with two added wings, and extensive 19th-century additions at the rear. Traditionally the site of Henry VIII's hunting kennels (hence the name), it was also the place used by city merchants as their exchange when plague struck London in 1603. A number of local tales about the *Dog* have grown up over the years. In the early 19th century it was a resort for well-to-do Londoners, and its tea gardens and cricket ground became famous. The last remnant of this open ground was built over in 1992. Despite large-scale renovation, the building nevertheless looks much the same today as it did in this turn of the century photograph.

The old Black Lion

83. The *Black Lion* in Plaistow is one of the claimants for the title of the oldest pub in Plaistow, and was noted as 'an old plastered house' in 1742. It survives to this day, though substantially rebuilt in 1875.

84. The *Greengate* in Barking Road, *c*.1900, also claimed to be the oldest pub in Plaistow, and dating back to at least 1776. Its old-fashioned weatherboard construction was once common in the area. In the middle of the 19th century, it was said that 'the *Greengate Inn* gave upon the marshes, and was the end of civilisation'. The pub was completely rebuilt in a modern style in 1953-4.

85. The *Abbey Arms*, Barking Road, was earlier known as the *Crown*. It was at least as old as 1742, though given a new Georgian front in 1820. The present building dates from 1882. Even after the building of the Barking Road in 1812, the *Abbey Arms* remained a very isolated building, which hardly seems credible now. Development really began *c*.1880, with the development of the Ireland's estate behind the pub.

86. The *Angel* in Church Street, West Ham, June 1902. The *Angel* was a timber-framed building of the 16th or 17th century; it was demolished in 1910.

Old Houses

Many large houses were built in West Ham when, in the 16th-18th centuries, the area was considered a pleasant rural retreat for wealthy city merchants. Almost none of these survive now, though several were still standing until the 1950s and 1960s.

Rokeby House, which stood in Stratford Broadway, was an early 17th-century building, re-fronted in the 18th century. It was an elegant seven-bay house, which towards the end of its life housed West Ham's first public library. The house was pulled down in 1898 to make way for the Stratford Empire theatre.

Upton House in Upton Lane (often confused with Ham House, which was earlier known as Upton House) was home to the Lister family, who were prominent Quakers; their most famous scion was Joseph (Lord) Lister, the pioneer of antiseptic surgery. The house was rebuilt in 1731 on a grand scale with a long classical frontage. It suffered demolition in 1968.

87. The Cedars, Portway. Adjacent to Ham House, it was occupied in the 19th century by Elizabeth Fry (1780-1845), the prison reformer. The philanthropist Samuel Gurney, who lived in Ham House, was her brother. King Frederic William IV of Prussia visited The Cedars in 1842 to meet Elizabeth Fry and, though the visit was a private one, the route was thronged with cheering crowds. Later the building became the headquarters for the 3rd Volunteer Battalion of the Essex Regiment. The Cedars was demolished in 1960.

Other large houses in Upton included Upton Cross Manor House, Red House (which still stands), and Grove House, all situated in or around Upton Lane.

Plaistow had a number of large gentlemen's residences, such as Richmond House, a fine five-bay, early 18th-century building, which was for a time the home of John Curwen. Porch House in Plaistow High Street was a most venerable building, old even in the 16th century. For much of its life it was home to the Rawstorne family, local landowners. Porch House was demolished in 1839.

Counts of hearths, required by the hearth tax and electoral registration, are a good indicator of property wealth, as larger properties obviously had more fireplaces. In the 17th century, Stratford and West Ham had a significant increase in the number of hearths, as the area became more fashionable.

In a predominantly agricultural community, there were of course also a number of farms, some farm-houses being of considerable antiquity.

The huge wave of Victorian house-building did produce some good quality houses for the middle classes, particularly in Forest Gate.

Many Victorian artisan houses survive, although the war and post-war slum clearances fortunately disposed of the most squalid of the many jerry-built properties thrown up during the late Victorian boom, particularly in the south of the borough. Some of the earliest municipal housing, built to high quality standards in 1899-1905, survives, such as Wise Road in Stratford.

88. Hyde House, a fine 16th-century mansion, once stood on the south side of Plaistow High Street. Demolished by 1811, it had been home to local worthies such as Sir Thomas Foot (1592-1688), merchant and Lord Mayor of London, and Aaron Hill (1685-1750), eccentric playwright and poet. Perhaps because the imposing arched gateway had the words 'This is the gate of everlasting life' carved on it, local tradition held that after the dissolution of Stratford Langthorne Abbey in 1538, the monks came to live at Hyde House.

89. Essex Lodge in Greengate Street was built, *c.*1840, re-using some architectural features from its predecessor, Essex House, a large Tudor building demolished in 1836.

90. Ham House was one of a number of fine mansions dating from the 16th century, originally known as Grove House or Rooke House. In the 18th century it was the residence of Dr. John Fothergill, the eminent naturalist, who converted the grounds into what were then one of the finest botanical gardens in Europe, with species from every part of the globe. Later, Ham House was occupied by the Gurney family, noted Quaker bankers and local philanthropists. John Gurney sold the 80-acre estate for £25,000 to the City of London Corporation so that they could turn it into a public park, the largest in West Ham. The house was demolished in 1872, and the park was opened to the public on 20 July 1874.

91. The Great Tithe Barn which stood next to Cumberland House, Plaistow. The building may have originally been the tithe barn of Stratford Langthorne Abbey, and was probably built in the 16th century. Though said to have been the largest in Essex, the barn was in fact similar in dimensions (31.6m long x 13m wide) to the surviving 13th-century Wheat Barn at Cressing. The barn had collapsed by 1905. Cumberland House was at least as old as the 17th century and took its name from the Duke of Cumberland (brother of George III) who owned the house 1787-90, and grazed his horses in the marshes nearby.

92. Broadway House, Plaistow Broadway, was demolished in 1882. A fine five-bay 18th-century house, it was the largest house in Plaistow. The property was owned by the Marten family in the early 19th century. Robert Marten (d.1839) was Plaistow's leading Baptist. His ecumenical views led Plaistow's Baptists into communion with the long-established Congregationalists, then an unusual arrangement which survived from 1812-69.

93. The tall house on the left of this drawing belonged at one time to the 'Unfortunate' Dr. Dodd, the curate of West Ham 1751-66, who was hanged for forgery in 1777. The building stood at the north end of Balaam Street. After his curacy in West Ham Dodd later enjoyed a spell of fame as a fashionable West End preacher. He has been described as 'a thorough ladies' man and an unctuous preacher; he had a great following and managed in a clever way to jumble up piety and dissipation'. Unfortunately he lived beyond his means and clumsily forged a cheque for £4,200. Forgery was then a hanging offence and, despite a large petition for clemency, he swung at Tyburn before a vast crowd.

Industries

Though it hardly seems credible now, West Ham was once described as 'The Factory Centre of the South of England'; it was a borough of heavy manufacturing industry, concentrated at Stratford and Silvertown. In 1910 there were over 335 constructional, engineering, and manufacturing concerns. We have already noted how Stratford had already become a proto-industrial centre in the late Middle Ages, with intensive milling, baking, slaughtering and leather-working activity. Silk weaving and calico printing later also became important, and there were serious riots in Stratford in 1675 when mechanical silk-weaving looms were introduced. The whole of the lower Lea valley in fact compares with, say, Coalbrookdale in Shropshire as a cradle of the Industrial Revolution, though the fact has been obscured because Lea-side became so heavily industrialised and remained industrialised for so long that little trace of the early stages now remain.

The key to West Ham's industrialisation was the ever-increasing demand from the Metropolis for processed goods of all kinds and their unwillingness to have noxious industries situated in their own area. Stratford, beyond the Lea, was ideal. One of the most fascinating

94. John Knight & Sons was formed in Silvertown in 1880, and was the first large-scale soap manufacturer in the area. In the early years, Knight's also made candles and other products needing tallow, but they later produced a wide range of quality toiletries, becoming world-famous for 'Knight's Castile' soap. Glycerine manufacture and oil refining were also important in the late Victorian and Edwardian periods. This pre-1900 photograph shows Russian oil barrels (wooden!) at Knight's own wharf, the Manhattan. The sign on the corrugated iron fence reads 'Manhattan Wharf: Wm Simpson & Co., Buyers & Exporters of Empty Petroleum Barrels'.

95. The main gate and general offices of Henry Tate & Son, *c.*1880. Sugar refining has been an important industry in Stratford and West Ham since the 1840s. Silvertown became the focus for sugar manufacture in the late Victorian period; Henry Tate arrived in 1877 and Abram Lyle in 1891. Tate's made cube sugar and Lyle's made golden syrup; the two firms amalgamated in 1921.

of these proto-industrial concerns was Thomas Frye's Bow China Works, at first founded on the Middlesex side of the Lea, but relocated in Stratford (i.e. on the Essex side) in 1749. Some of the finest pieces were produced 1750-7, and many are now in the collections of the Victoria & Albert and British Museums, with a good selection also at the Passmore Edwards Museum.

Although materials of practically every imaginable kind have been made in Stratford and West Ham, there were particular products for which the area was noted. Chemicals and pharmaceuticals were particularly important, sulphuric acid manufacture, oil refining, toiletries and disinfectants, paints, dyes and inks being merely among the most notable. The rendering down of animal fat into glue, fertiliser, soap and tallow was a particularly noxious trade and, after being banned from London in the 1840s, a number of firms moved to the area. The stench of Stratford, particularly near the Lea, was a standing, if grim, joke among older locals. Odams in Silvertown made manure out of liquid blood, and needed a slaughterhouse adjacent to supply the 'raw material'. John Knight's works nearby made soap and a wide variety of by-products. Sugar-refining was carried out in Stratford and later in Silvertown, an area still dominated by the giant Tate & Lyle works. Heavy industry was represented by the Thames Ironworks, which built several of London's bridges as well as warships, and the Stratford Railway works. The supply of building materials was also important. Printing was a significant local industry and, in Silvertown, the settlement was dominated by the rubber works of S. W. Silver & Co.

The post-war period has seen much of this industry move out or close down, and the docks' closure seems to locals to seal the area's fate. Little manufacturing industry is now carried on in West Ham, although there has been some influx of service industries recently.

96. A publicity photograph showing products made at Tate's, prior to the 1921 amalgamation with Lyle's. Tate was a philanthropist as well as an industrialist, and not only founded a Tate Institute in Silvertown to provide social and educational facilities for Tate workers but, more famously, established the Tate Gallery in London.

97. Tate's workers endured hard conditions when this photograph was taken in 1917. They worked in terrific heat and were subject to painful 'sugar boils' on the body as a result of constant contact with raw sugar. Wages averaged 21s. a week. Raw cane sugar from the West Indies was unloaded direct from ship to factory on conveyor belts and melted for refining immediately. The most arduous tasks were undertaken by 14 to 18-year-old boy-labourers. However, there were always crowds outside the factory gates hoping to be taken on.

98. Stratford Railway Works. This photograph, dating from 1891, shows the Great Eastern Railway's Erecting Shop at their Stratford Works. A repair depot was already operating here under the Eastern Counties Railway in 1839, and by 1847 the main works had been transferred from Romford. This was during the heyday of the 'Railway King', George Hudson and, before a financial scandal ruined his reputation, the area around the works was called Hudson Town. The works covered 78 acres, incorporating a carriage works, printing works, and laboratory and employed over 6,000 men, building and repairing hundreds of locomotives. The works were closed in 1963.

99. Stratford Railway Works achieved a still-unbeaten world record with this G.E.R. locomotive, No. 930. This was the fastest-built steam locomotive ever, constructed in only 9 hours 47 minutes by a team of 85 men on 10-11 December 1891. No. 930 gave over 40 years of service, running for more than a million miles before being scrapped in 1935.

100. The great shipbuilding company of Thames Ironworks was situated on both sides of Bow Creek, though the actual ship construction was carried out on the West Ham side of the river. Founded in 1846 by C. J. Mare (1815-98), the company built the Navy's first ironclad ship, the *Warrior*, in 1860. The Ironworks later came under the directorship of Arnold Hills (1857-1927), the founder of West Ham United F.C. As well as building several dozen major battleships for the world's navies, the 'Thames' also manufactured the iron work for Blackfriars and Hammersmith Bridges. This photograph from 1901 shows H.M.S. *Duncan* ready for launch. The works closed down in 1912 in the face of competition from the shipyards of the Tyne and Wear.

101. The launch of H.M.S. *Thunderer* on 1 February 1911. At that time the largest dreadnought battleship afloat, *Thunderer* displaced 22,500 tons and was armed with 13½-inch (34cm) guns. She was the last warship to be built at the 'Thames'.

102. Rubber and gutta percha manufacture was an important Stratford industry in the middle of the 19th century, but rapidly became overshadowed by the scale of production at the India Rubber, Gutta Percha and Telegraph Works Co., founded near North Woolwich in 1852 by Stephen W. Silver. The whole area soon became known as Silvertown. The works were on a very large scale, covering 17 acres and employing over 4,000 people. In its early years, the works were famous for the production of submarine telegraphic cable, then a technological marvel. The works were demolished in the 1960s and an industrial estate built on the site. This advertisement dates from 1955.

103. Victoria Dock under construction, 1854. There were small docks and wharves along the Lea at Stratford and West Ham from the 15th century. The rising population and booming trade of mid-Victorian London necessitated a rapid expansion of dock facilities, and the new large steamships needed bigger docks for loading and unloading than the old sailing ships. A number of schemes were put forward to improve London's docks, and in 1843 land on the Plaistow and East Ham Levels was bought up cheaply by the North Woolwich Land Co. The railway to North Woolwich opened four years later, and plans were put in hand for the construction of the Royal Victoria Dock. The work was made easier as the marsh lies below sea level, enabling the docks walls to be banked up rather than excavated (a costlier option). When the Victoria (later Royal Victoria) Dock was opened in 1855 it was the first to be served directly by rail. The prime movers behind the scheme were the entrepreneurs, Morton Peto, Edward Betts and Thomas Brassey, whilst the mathematical genius, George Parker Bidder, presided over the design.

104. Steam and hydraulic power was used throughout the Royal Docks—the first docks to be so equipped. This engraving shows the hydraulic lift used for ship repair in the Pontoon Dock next to the Royal Victoria Dock.

105. A contemporary humorous cartoon about the use of steam-power in excavations for the Royal Albert Dock, 1876. A steam land-dredger was used, much to the excitement of locals. The sketched background depicts the houses and factories of North Woolwich and Beckton gasworks with some accuracy.

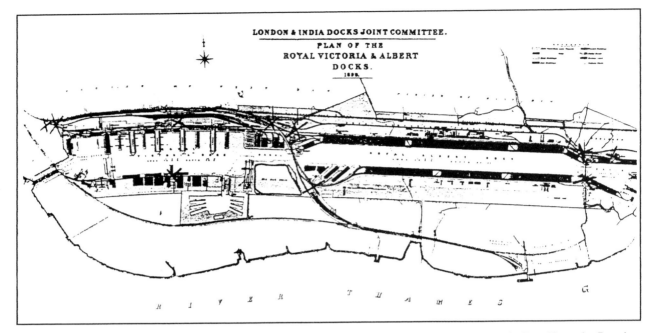

106. The Royal Albert Dock was opened in June 1880 by the Duke of Connaught. Lying partly in East Ham, the Royal Albert completed the most advanced docks system in the Empire, further added to by the King George V Dock in 1921. Together, the Victoria and Albert Docks contained 175 acres of water with seven miles of quays.

107. Crockett's Leather Cloth Co. built a factory in Abbey Road in the 1850s, and traded very profitably from what was for some time a monopoly supply position. Older residents—mostly female—recall the workers in the inter-war years streaming out of the factory absolutely covered in cotton fluff, a by-product of the cotton milling process carried on in the factory.

108. A 1955 advertisement for Dane & Co., founded in 1853. Stratford was an important centre for the manufacture of paints, varnishes, dyes and printing inks, and many of the firms producing inks gravitated to Sugar House Lane, Stratford, where Dane's still operates.

Transport

Stratford's function as gateway to the capital really began *c*.1115, when Queen Maud built Bow Bridge, Channelsea Bridge and the causeway across the braid of Lea back rivers to join Middlesex to Essex. The old Roman Road to Colchester via Old Ford was effectively bypassed and the new more southerly route had better access to the City. As the last river crossing before the city, Stratford became a natural stopping place and point of trade. As has been previously noted, the early focus of trade was cattle and grain, and a weekly market and annual fair at West Ham from the 13th century may have encouraged other traders. The main network of roads connecting the settlements of Stratford, West Ham and Plaistow was probably of great antiquity. Before the arrival of mechanised transport, the area was served by coaches and carriers; the Great East Road through Stratford to East Anglia was always a major trade route, bringing in sheep and woollen products as well as cattle and grain from that fertile area.

Stratford was a pioneering base for the operation of steam carriages. From his works in Stratford High Street, Walter Hancock patented a coke-fired steam engine in 1827 small enough to be fitted to road vehicles. He began building 'horseless carriages'—some of the earliest manufactured in Britain—and operated these steam coaches to and around London during the 1830s. Understandably he was bitterly opposed by those who profited from the horse trade—such as coachmen, ostlers and turnpike authorities—and he abandoned the enterprise, *c*.1840.

By this time the railway had arrived, to transform Stratford and reinforce its status as a transport node. The station and railway works were built in 1839, part of what was to become the Great Eastern Railway. Greatly expanded in the reign of George Hudson, 'The Railway King', Stratford station and its works were the strategic centre of a rail network carrying traffic from Essex and East Anglia into and out of London, to and from Docklands, up and down the Lea Valley, and through the capital's northern suburbs on what we now call the North London Line.

After several years of decline, particularly since the closure of the railway works in 1963, Stratford has revived as a rail hub. The refurbishment of the North London line and the building of the Docklands Light Railway have both meant increased traffic, and three further significant construction projects will confirm Stratford's position. These are, the extension of the Jubilee Line from central London to Stratford via Docklands; the CrossRail project, providing a new trans-London link from Paddington to Stratford and beyond; and the routing of the high-speed Channel Tunnel rail link through Stratford via an international station there.

Public road transport improved as the population boomed. The first horse-tram from Stratford to London ran in 1870, and in the 1870s and 1880s experiments were being made with steam, compressed air and electric traction. It was not, however, until after 1903 when the West Ham municipal authorities took over the tram service that electrification of all tram routes was achieved. Local control was retained until 1933, when the London Passenger Transport Board was formed. The end of the tram era came just before the Second World

War; Mayor Daisy Parsons drove West Ham's first trolley-bus in 1937. The trolley-bus was in turn consigned to the scrap-heap in 1960, replaced by the ordinary motor-bus. Motor omnibus services had started in West Ham by 1906 and quickly replaced the old horse-bus routes.

With the opening of the Victoria Dock in 1855, West Ham became a major seaport. The location of Stratford and West Ham on a strategic bend in the Thames and beside the tidal Lea encouraged river traffic, and Stratford had its own dock from 1821, while other wharves on the Lea back rivers were older. With the establishment of major industries along the Thames in the mid- and late-Victorian periods, wharves crowded together on the waterfront. The addition of the Royal Albert Dock in 1880 and the King George V Dock in 1921 made this Royal Group of Docks the lynch-pin of the Port of London Authority and its predecessors, and there were grandiose plans for an even larger dock on the north side of the Royal Albert Dock. However, Tilbury Dock gradually grew in importance, and, following containerisation, for which the Royal Docks were not equipped, the decline and closure of the 'Royals' was inevitable. Following some regeneration in Docklands, the first Thames passenger boat service—the RiverBus—was started in the late 1980s between West Ham and Chelsea with various stops en route.

Part of the regeneration has included the building of London City Airport on redundant dock land partly in West Ham. The airport was opened in the mid-1980s and serves mainly business passengers.

109. Plaistow Station, c.1902. Opened in 1858, the station lay on the new direct route between London and Southend which replaced an earlier more circuitous route via Forest Gate and Tilbury. Between c.1876-1934 there was a small railway works beside the station, operated by the London, Tilbury and Southend Railway and its successors.

110. Upton Park Station, *c*.1902, stands on the West Ham side of Green Street, and was opened by the London, Tilbury and Southend Railway in 1877.

111. The London, Tilbury & Southend Railway was built between Forest Gate and Tilbury in 1854, and extended to Southend two years later (the now-familiar route into Fenchurch Street via Bow did not come into operation until a few years later). Most of the L.T.S.R. locomotive fleet received names from stations and localities along the line's route. This 4-4-2T loco, No.15, was *East Ham*, built in 1881 and scrapped in 1932. The L.T.S.R. operated a large number of these standardised workhorses hauling a variety of traffic, and they were known as the 'Tilbury Universal Machines'.

112. Tidal Basin swing bridge, looking south, April 1904. This notorious traffic bottleneck stood at the western end of the Royal Victoria Dock where both road and railway had to cross a busy dock exit. Shipping had priority, so there were frequent delays while the swing bridge was swung to allow shipping in or out. Extra time always had to be allowed by anyone journeying north or south of the docks, and 'catching a bridger' was a common excuse for lateness.

113. The Channelsea river, *c*.1900, looking south from Abbey Mills. A very dreary scene! The numerous back rivers of the Lea at Stratford were reputedly built by King Alfred the Great in 895 to divert the Lea and trap a marauding Danish fleet. However, it is more likely that they originated a century or so later as mill streams. The rivers are all tidal and at one time generated considerable barge traffic.

114. An experimental battery-powered tram worked the Greengate-Canning Town Station route for a few years from about 1889-92.

115. West Ham's electric tramways were inaugurated on 27 February 1904, following the obtaining from Parliament in 1898-1900 of the relevant powers. This photograph shows the first tram about to leave the depot.

WEST HAM CORPORATION TRAMWAYS
Support Your Trams

Travel by the Latest Type "Pullman" Car, the Smooth Riding Qualities of which Assure Passengers of the Maximum Ease and Comfort.

Luxuriously Upholstered.   Efficiently Lighted and Ventilated.

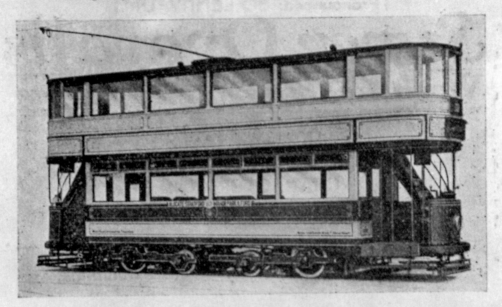

116. Car No. 63, West Ham Corporation Tramways. By 1928, West Ham's trams were fully enclosed and a great source of civic pride, as this advertisement indicates. The livery was a rich chocolate brown and cream. Local control ended in 1933 when the London Passenger Transport Board took control of all metropolitan services.

1. LONDON TRANSPORT ROAD SERVICES

("500" and "600" numbers are electric trolleybuses. "700" numbers are Green Line Coaches: the remaining numbers indicate Central area motor omnibuses).

Table "A"—Summary of Services from London (Aldgate)

	To and from Stratford Broadway	To and from Canning Town Station and Barking Road.
Weekdays	10, 25 and 96 661 and 663 720, 721 and 722	23 and 40 567 and 665 723, 723A
Weekdays, peak hours only		15 (run all day Sat.) 565 (NOT Sat.) 569 (then to North Woolwich)
Sundays	10 and 25 661 and 663 720, 721 and 722	9, 15, 23A and 40 567 and 665 723, 723A
Night service	298	295 (NOT Sat. night/Sun. morning)

Table "B"—Summary of Direct Services Eastward and Northward

	To and from Stratford Broadway	To and from Canning Town Stn.		To and from Stratford Broadway	To and from Canning Town Stn.
Abridge	10	—	Hornchurch	86a, 722	—
Becontree	258, 722	23, 106, 175	Ilford	25, 86a, 663	—
Bp. Stortford	720	—	Loughton	720	—
Brentwood	721	—	Rainham	—	723 723a
Chadwell H ath	86a, 695 721	—			
			Redbridge	96	—
Chigwell	10	—	Romford	86a, 721	175
Chingford Mt.	697,699	—	Staplefd. Abbts.	—	175
Dagenham	—	175, 723, 723a	Tilbury	—	723
			Upminster	86a, 722	—
Epping	720	—	Walthamstow	697, 699	685
Grays	—	723	Wanstead	96	40
Harlow	720	—	Woodford	720	—

2. LONDON TRANSPORT RAIL SERVICES

Central Line: From Ealing Broadway or West Ruislip via Liverpool Street to Stratford Main Station; and thence to Epping via Woodford; or, Hainault via Wanstead and Newbury Park.

117. An interesting summary of bus services from Stratford in 1955.

Social Life

Despite much poverty, the crowded streets of Stratford and West Ham have generated a rich social life which perhaps reached its peak between the wars. Sporting prowess has been particularly important, no more so than at West Ham United F.C., whose fortunes have often been taken as a metaphor for the vicissitudes of the whole area. Founded in 1900, the club in its familiar claret and blue strip has enjoyed a loyal following locally, if only moderate success in terms of winning cups and championships. They won the F.A. Cup in 1963-4, 1974-5, and 1979-80, and the European Cup Winners' Cup in 1964-5. In 1993-4 the team were promoted to the new Premier Division.

In the last century the *Spotted Dog* in Upton was well-known for its cricket matches, and was subsequently home to Clapton F.C., who still occupy the adjacent 'Spotted Dog' Ground. West Ham Stadium in Custom House was home to a successful circus of speedway stars in the inter-war years; their names are commemorated in a number of street-names adopted when the stadium was demolished for housing in 1978.

Boxing has always been an important sport in the area, and its history locally can be traced back to illegal prize-fighting contests on the marshes in the 18th and 19th centuries. Boxing often ran in families. Between the wars, notable local fighters were the Thakes, Alec and Jim, of Canning Town, George and Ginger Merrit of Silvertown, the Lee brothers, Jimmy, Leo and Tommy, also of Canning Town; all national class boxers, some competing at international level.

Generous provision of swimming facilities by the local authorities ensured the success of local swimming clubs at national level; E. H. Temme, the first man to swim the Channel in both directions, lived at Tidal Basin.

In other words, there was a welter of sporting talent; a local Baptist minister saw, in the late 1960s, three England captains in one day in Plaistow. These were Bobby Moore, captain of the England football squad, David Sheppard, former England cricket captain (then working at the Mayflower Centre, a Canning Town philanthropic institute), and Chester Barnes, England table tennis captain.

Theatres, music-halls and cinemas all enjoyed great popularity. Of the theatres in Stratford, which included the Theatre Royal, the Borough and the Empire, only the Theatre Royal survives and, of the score of picture-palaces which once attracted such huge crowds, none are still in use as cinemas. The Broadway Cinema in Stratford's Tramway Avenue was the largest in Britain when it opened in 1927. Stratford has also been a home for music; the Stratford Music Festival, founded in 1882, and still in existence, was an important showcase for local talent. Interest in music was stimulated by the presence of some high-quality academies of music, and, in the last century, the presence of the Curwen family. John Curwen (1816-80) invented the tonic sol-fa system of musical notation which enabled large numbers of people who could not read ordinary musical scores to become accomplished performers. The Stratford Central Library in Water Lane has also been an important focus for social activity, its staff being instrumental in founding the Newham Libraries Music Circle and the Newham History Society, both still thriving. Close by, the Passmore Edwards Museum is still home to the Essex Field Club, the leading natural history organisation in Essex and Metropolitan Essex.

Of course, social life also encompasses ambience and lifestyle. Communities were close-knit before the Second World War, and there was a sense of collective struggle in facing up to the hardships of life. These close-knit communities are well recalled by older residents, and were to be found throughout the borough of West Ham; to name a Stratford example only, the Carpenters estate around Carpenters Road was a memorable instance of this attitude, where everyone seemed to know everybody else (and their business!) and the local parade of shops in Lett Road served as a bush telegraph for news.

Entertainment was often free, derived from the passing scenes of street life. In Stratford, for instance, there was the Turkey Rhubarb Man, who, dressed as a Turk, would tout rhubarb round the streets calling 'For sick headaches and pains in the stomach, the root is best and not the branch!'. Acrobats would often perform on Sunday mornings, and the piano-organ man had a regular round. Processions made an interesting spectacle; the biggest in Stratford were the annual May Day parade, and the Fairlop Fair procession on the first Friday in July, which passed through Stratford on its way to Fairlop.

118. West Ham United, 1900-1, their first professional season. The origins of the team lay in three amateur sides: The Old Castle Swifts, employees of the Union Castle Steamship Line; St Luke's Football Club, founded at the Canning Town church of that name, and the Thames Ironworks Football Club. The Swifts amalgamated with St Luke's, and Thames Ironworks disbanded in 1899 because of high costs. However, Arnold Hills, owner of Thames Ironworks, made a large donation to ensure the formation of a professional football club, and West Ham United Football Company Ltd. was founded on 5 July 1900. The team originally played at West Ham Memorial Ground but, because this was inconveniently located, the club moved to the present Boleyn Ground—which actually lies in East Ham—in 1904.

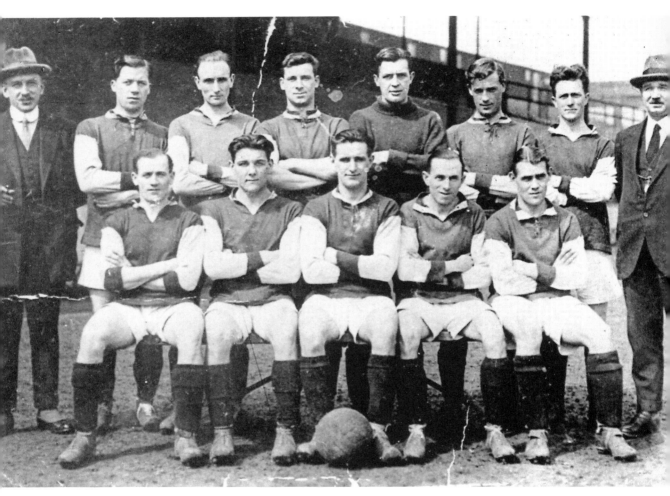

119. West Ham United 1922-3. The team was promoted to the First Division in 1923 and also reached the cup final. The final was the first to be played at Wembley Stadium, and went down in history for the 'Policeman on a White Horse' incident. Over 150,000 turned up to see the match, and the crowds spilled onto the pitch, to be marshalled back behind the touch-line by a lone policeman, P.C. Scorey, on a white horse. He achieved instant fame as photographs of the event appeared in newspapers all round the world. The match was started after a delay of 40 minutes, and West Ham lost 2-0 to Bolton Wanderers. However, the team still toured the borough in a decorated tram afterwards, cheered on by huge crowds.

120. The Borough Theatre in Stratford High Street opened in 1896. Seating over 3,000, it was by far the largest theatre in Essex and in size outranked most West End playhouses. The greatest actors have played here, including Sir Henry Irving, Ellen Terry, and Beerbohm Tree. Designed by Frank Matcham for Albert Fredericks (also owner of Stratford's Theatre Royal), the Borough remained in the hands of the Fredericks family until 1933, when it was converted into a cinema. It survived as the 'Rex' until 1969 and now stands derelict after a spell as a bingo hall. This photograph was taken around the time of the theatre's opening in 1896, with shops still to let along the High Street frontage and hoardings advertising a forthcoming performance by 'Mr. Tree'.

121. A National Cycling Union meet at the West Ham Memorial Ground in 1903. Cycling was an enormously popular pastime, particularly in the Edwardian period and between the wars, with many flourishing clubs holding organised outings to the countryside. Epping Forest in particular was a popular destination.

122. West Ham Park; the Portway entrance, *c*.1905. Following the opening of the park to the public in 1874, a stone cairn was built to mark the site of Ham House, demolished in 1872. As West Ham's largest park, this 'Green Lung' was an important recreational resource for the area.

123. An advertisement for a hospital ball at Stratford Town Hall. Although a 28-bed hospital had been paid for by the philanthropist Passmore Edwards in 1895, public subscription contributed to the extension of the hospital in 1906-10. It was renamed Queen Mary's Hospital in 1916 when Her Majesty became patron.

124. North West Ham Athletic and Boxing Club, c.1926. Like many deprived areas, West Ham had a considerable tradition of boxing, stretching back to the days of illegal prize-fighting on the marsh. Victorian boxer Jem Mace (1831-1910), world heavyweight champion, lived in Hamfrith Road. This photograph shows a gallery of inter-war boxing stars from the club with their awards. From left to right: A. E. Ilett, Senior (Hon. Sec.), F. Power (British 6-stone champion 1926), A. E. Ilett, Junior (British 7-stone champion 1924, runner-up 1925), Wright Cundy (Patron), George Davis (President), W. Oldershaw (Chairman), A. Foster (British 8-stone champion 1925, runner-up 1924), J. Stannard (Instructor), and A. Foster, Senior (Hon. Treasurer).

Entertainments, Meetings, &c.

Town Hall, Stratford.

WEST HAM HOSPITAL BALL,
1898.

The Ninth Annual Ball in aid of this Hospital will take place on

Wednesday, 26th January, 1898,
. . AT THE ABOVE HALL . .

Dancing will commence at 8.30 p.m.
Carriages may be ordered for 2 to 2.30 a.m.
Pool's Band has been Engaged.

ADMISSION BY TICKET ONLY:—

Single Tickets (including Light Refreshments).. **7/6**
Double   ,,   ,,   ,, (Admitting
Lady and Gentleman or Two Ladies) .. .. **12/6.**

TICKETS TO BE OBTAINED FROM H. C. Cowles, Esq.
37, Broadway, Stratford ; J. M. Goldie, Esq., Falloden, Norwich Road, Forest Gate ; Fred. E. Harris, Esq., Town Hall, West Ham ; Ald. G. Hay, J.P., "The Chestnuts," Stratford ; H. Hollingsworth, Esq., 67, Claremont Road, Forest Gate ; F. G. Rayment, Esq., 54, Chaucer Road, Upton, Forest Gate ; J. Lovegrove, Esq., "Monte Christo," Richmond Gardens, Forest Gate (Hon. Sec.); L. D. Rea, The Hospital (Hon. Sec.); or from any member of the Ball Committee.

125. A concert at Stratford Town Hall, 1896. Stratford and West Ham have a long musical tradition; John Curwen created the tonic sol-fa system of musical notation and founded the Tonic Sol-Fa College to promote the concept. His son, J. Spencer Curwen, founded the Stratford Music Festival.

126. Beckton Road Park, shortly after opening in 1894. More correctly known as Canning Town Recreation Ground, the park was, together with Balaam Street Recreation Ground in Plaistow, West Ham's earliest municipal park. The grounds stood on the corner of Prince Regent Lane and Beckton Road (now Newham Way) and were an important recreational resource for Canning Town.

127. With its great network of docks and labour-hungry industry, West Ham was a natural focus for immigration. Its major industries attracted Germans, Irish and Scots, whilst the port facilities were a magnet for Chinese, Indians (known as Lascars), and Caribbean seamen, many of whom settled. Canning Town had the largest black community in the Metropolitan area from very early this century. In the depression after the First World War many blacks faced unemployment and racism. To ease their plight, a Ceylonese Methodist, Pastor Kamal Chunchie, opened this Coloured Men's Institute in Tidal Basin Road.

128. Christmas party at the Coloured Men's Institute in 1926, showing races from every corner of the British Empire.

129. There was a good deal of philanthropic work undertaken in Stratford and Docklands, much of it carried out by the great public schools and university colleges. Some of this charitable work took the form of 'settlements', permanent bases for good works. One of the best known was the Docklands Settlement. This began life in 1894 as a mission from Malvern College. The mission was set on a sound footing by (Sir) Reginald Kennedy-Cox (d.1966) who sank much of his own personal fortune in the development of the settlement. This drawing shows the chapel of St George & St Helena, built in 1930. The settlement was reorganised in 1957 by Rev. (later Bishop) David Sheppard, and renamed the Mayflower Centre.

Education

As with the rest of the country, education in Stratford and West Ham originated with the charity schools of the 18th century, usually associated with the established church, and supplemented by 'dame-schools' of dubious educational quality. The earliest school in West Ham was founded in 1723 at All Saints, the parish church, as a result of a bequest by one Mary Battailhey. This was followed by another charity school founded in 1766 through a bequest from Sarah Bonnell. The 19th century saw an increase in educational provision through the rival 'British' and 'National' school systems; voluntary schools provided by the nonconformist and established churches respectively. These schools provided elementary education using the monitor system, in which older pupils taught the younger, and most learning was by rote.

A British School was built at Salway Place, in association with Brickfields Congregational chapel in 1806-8, whilst another was founded in Plaistow, c.1820. A National School was also set up in Plaistow in 1830, in association with St Mary's church, and in Stratford a National School was opened in the Sunday School Room of St John's Church in 1835, followed by another in 1850. This was the Christ Church National School, connected with Christ Church, Stratford High Street (now demolished). Some of the schools made valiant attempts to serve desperately poor areas; Holy Trinity National School, Canning Town, began life as a class in a leaky shed in Hallsville Road in 1848; in wet weather the teacher had to raise an umbrella! Chapel Street Ragged School in Stratford, founded in 1851, followed the principles of the Ragged School Union which offered a very basic education for the children of those in deepest poverty, usually in the form of vocational training; for instance, girls were given domestic training and boys taught to shoe-shine.

The provision of education, however was woefully inadequate as the population boomed in West Ham. In 1870, the Education Act permitted local authorities to form school boards and to supplement independent provision with board schools. In the face of intense clerical opposition, West Ham was one of the first districts to establish a school board, in 1871. The board immediately began a comprehensive programme of school building to ensure elementary education for all. True secondary education did not get under way until 1906 with the opening of the West Ham Municipal Secondary School. Both the Hadow Report of 1926 and the 1944 Education Act reorganised education which resulted in further secondary provision. Comprehensive education was introduced in 1972. Stratford was at the forefront of political argument over the future of education in 1990-1 when Stratford School, Upton Lane, 'opted out' of local authority control, becoming one of the first schools to adopt direct central government funding, known as grant-maintained status. The disputes caused during this process in Stratford made national headlines.

Higher education provision began in 1898 when West Ham Technical Institute (later Municipal College) opened in Romford Road, Stratford. After the war, the name was changed again to West Ham College of Technology, then in 1970 it became part of North East London Polytechnic. University status, with the title 'University of East London' was achieved in 1992.

130. Abbey Road Board School stood in Abbey Road, West Ham until its closure in 1938. This picture was taken in 1885. The school opened in 1881 for 900 children, but had to be expanded several times until it accommodated 1,660 children. This sort of overcrowding was a familiar problem for many schools in the borough in the early years of the school board. In 1870 there were only 8,000 school places in West Ham, though by 1902 there was capacity for 60,000 children. Abbey Road School was demolished in 1946.

131. West Ham Church School was founded at the church in 1723. This photograph shows a class in 1897. Closely associated with Sarah Bonnell's charity school, it was enlarged and reorganised several times, and is still in existence.

132. A delightful scene from a classroom at Napier Road School, West Ham. This photograph dates from shortly after the opening of the school in 1904; it was built to serve the Manor Road area. The photograph is a very good record of working-class children's clothing at the turn of the century. Note the caged bird in the front row.

133. New City Road School in Plaistow, *c.*1913. This massive yellow-brick three-storey school was opened in 1897 to serve the boomimg Bemersyde estate, with a capacity of no less than 1,560 pupils.

134. South Hallsville Board School in 1897. The school was opened in 1878 in Agate Street, Tidal Basin. The Hallsville area of Canning Town was desperately poor. By the Second World War, the school had been enlarged and rebuilt several times, but early in the Blitz there was an appalling tragedy. The school received a direct hit as local families were sheltering there, awaiting evacuation, and 73 people were killed in the disaster.

135. The Eastern Counties (later Great Eastern) Railway established a Mechanics' Institution in Angel Lane, in 1851, shown in this engraving. A variety of vocational and technical classes were held at the institute, and lessons and a large library improved literacy among the company's workforce. A number of philanthropic organisations opened similar educational institutes in the area, notably, Tate's in Silvertown where the Tate Institute was built in 1887, and the Carpenters' Institute, which had been established a year earlier in Stratford.

136. West Ham School Board, 95 The Grove. Built in 1897, these offices housed several council departments. The building has now been replaced with a modern office block also housing council offices.

Worthies

Many and varied talents have come out of Stratford and the surrounding areas, and the following illustrations are only a small selection of the famous names associated with West Ham. Other worthies are mentioned elsewhere in this book.

Luke Howard (1772-1864) was a chemist who founded a major pharmaceutical company. Established in Plaistow in 1797, the firm became Howard & Sons when it moved to Stratford in 1805, and remained there until it moved to Ilford in 1914. Howard was also a pioneering meteorologist who made daily climatic observations and gave cloud formations, such as *cirrus* and *cumulus*, their modern names. The land-owning Pelly family loom large in any history of West Ham; Sir John Pelly, Bt. (1777-1852), a governor of the Hudson's Bay Company, was a noted local philanthropist, while Canon Richard Pelly (vicar of West Ham 1891-1916) was well-known for his charitable works.

Joseph (Lord) Lister (1827-1912) was the founder of modern antiseptic surgery; he was born at Upton House, Upton Lane. The poet Gerard Manley Hopkins (1844-89) was born at a house in The Grove, Stratford, and the mystical writer and pioneering dietician Anna Kingsford (1846-88), founder of the occult Hermetic Society, was also born in Stratford.

More recent worthies include the actor and comedian Stanley Holloway (1890-1982), who was educated in Stratford, and Dame Anna Neagle (1904-1986), who lived in Upton Lane.

137. Aaron Hill (1688-1750), poet and playwright, lived in Plaistow. Noted eccentric, his plays were regarded as outlandish, and he was frequently involved in bizarre schemes, including one for extracting oil from beech-mast. At his Plaistow house, he planted a vineyard and made 'wine' from the resulting grapes though, as he had neglected to ferment the juice, the product was undrinkable.

138. George Edwards (1693-1773) was a pioneering naturalist who lived in Plaistow. His four-volume book, *The History of Birds*, was at the time the most comprehensive work on ornithology, and was later supplemented by three volumes of *Gleanings in Natural History*. All seven publications contained hand-coloured engravings—nearly 600 in all—and now, of course, very rare.

139. Edmund Burke (1729-97), the great Georgian statesman, lived in Plaistow from 1759-61.

140. Elizabeth Fry (1780-1845) was born in Norfolk, a member of the Gurney family, who were bankers and leading Quakers. For much of her life, she lived at The Cedars, Portway, in West Ham, where she received the King of Prussia on a private visit in 1842. Her philanthropic work is of course very well known, particularly her improvements to the conditions of prisoners in the infamous Newgate. She also worked to improve the lot of vagrants, beggars, and convicts transported to Australia. She travelled widely in Europe to promote prison improvements.

141. John Curwen (1816-80) was the founder of the Tonic Sol-Fa system of musical notation which taught millions to sing and play musical instruments simply and without the need to learn crotchets and quavers. He was minister of the Congregational chapel at Plaistow from 1844-64, and was active in local politics, as well as being a member of West Ham School Board from 1871. He founded the Curwen Press in 1862, which originally printed music but later turned to high-quality art printing, and established the Tonic Sol-Fa College in 1870. The building still stands in Earlham Grove, Forest Gate. The College was later run by Curwen's son, J. Spencer Curwen, and then converted into the Metropolitan Academy of Music by his successors Harding Bonner and Frank Bonner. Curwen was noted for the tenacity of his views, which often brought him into conflict with others in authority.

142. Father Samuel Catton was a well-known character in mid-Victorian Plaistow. A Quaker and a pharmacist, his shop sold not only medicines but also drapery, ironmongery and sweets. A forceful campaigner in the temperance cause, he was known as 'Father' Catton because he befriended the children of the area and, in his Quaker garb of broad-brimmed hat, high collar and white neck-cloth, he delighted them with magic-lantern shows. From these eager bands he managed to recruit a 'Junior Temperance Society', and also raised a public subscription to build a Temperance Hall.

143. Edith Kerrison (1850-1934) was the first woman to be elected to West Ham council, and devoted her life to public service. She was a councillor from 1917-26, and alderman from 1926-34. A trained nurse, she worked in the Albert Dock Hospital, and later ran a co-operative home for young men in the Barking Road. She was also active on the Board of Guardians, and the council's public health, education, and libraries committee.

Politics

Out of the crowded streets of Stratford and West Ham grew a strong movement for socialism and trade unionism, born out of unemployment, the casual labour system, and poor living conditions. Early socialist factions such as the Social Democratic Federation had some success in recruiting locally, and Keir Hardie was elected to serve as MP for South West Ham in 1892, the first true Labour member of Parliament of Parliament. In 1898 an alliance of socialists and progressives formed a Labour group which campaigned vigorously, and secured a majority of seats on West Ham council. This was the first local council in the country to be Labour-controlled, and they continued the policy of public works started as early as 1886 when the council was first formed. Scare stories about socialism ensured the defeat of the Labour group by a Municipal Alliance in 1900. Up until the First World War, control see-sawed between Labour and Alliance, then in 1919 Labour won a majority of seats and retained control until 1965 when the London Borough of Newham was created. Labour have always held a majority in Newham.

Following Keir Hardie's success in South West Ham, the Conservatives briefly regained the seat, but from 1906 Will Thorne held it until 1918, transferring to the new Plaistow seat which he held until 1945. Between 1918-48 West Ham was divided into four seats (Plaistow, Silvertown, Stratford and Upton), then reduced again to two. Plaistow and Silvertown were Labour-held from 1918 onwards, Stratford was Labour-held from 1922 onwards, while better-off Upton swung between Labour and Conservative until 1934. Since that time, West Ham has returned only Labour members of Parliament.

The worst problem facing the civic authorities was the relief of poverty caused by unemployment; technically this was a matter for the poor law union, but it inevitably involved the borough, too. Unemployment was so severe in West Ham in the 1920s that the poor law guardians repeatedly overspent their allocation of funds. This led central government to replace the locally-elected guardians in 1926 with a nominated board which cut benefits. Such action was bitterly unpopular locally and had long-lasting repercussions.

One of the chief causes of job insecurity was the system of casual labour and piece-work labour used by many employers in local industries. Most notorious was the 'call-on' system in the Docks, where would-be employees had to stand outside the dock gates and literally fight to be picked by the overseers. This system (known locally as 'on the stones' because it involved waiting on the cobblestones at the dock entrances) is recalled with great resentment by older locals, and contributed to the ferocious protectionism of dockers' unions after the war.

The 'new unionism' of the 1880s and 1890s had received widespread local support. The Gas Workers and General Labourers Union (now the G.M.B.) had been founded in Canning Town in 1889 by Will Thorne, and the dockers' strike of 1888 received hearty local support. Other unions representing unskilled workers such as the Tea Operatives Union found the area a fertile recruiting ground. Many of the early union leaders, such as Will Thorne and

Jack Jones, went on to successful political careers in the local council and as parliamentarians. The General Strike of 1926 was well-supported locally, thanks partly to indignation about the government's handling of poor-law relief.

The Stratford Co-operative Society, founded in 1861, was one of the first in the south of England, and was the forerunner of the London Co-operative Society. The difficult social conditions in the area also made popular numerous mutual benefit societies and friendly societies.

144. West Ham became a municipal borough in 1886, and this photograph shows the first borough council, elected to serve from 1886-7. The first mayor was J. Meeson (seated, centre). Becoming a county borough just three years later in 1889, the council oversaw enormous growth and change. In 1898, the council became the first in the country to have a Labour majority.

145. Keir Hardie (1856-1915) made history in 1892 by becoming the first true Labour member of Parliament. Son of a Scottish miner, Hardie had been active in Scottish politics for some time before being adopted as Labour candidate for the West Ham South constituency. He beat the Conservative candidate in a straight fight, backed by an alliance of trade unionists, liberals, nonconformists and Roman Catholics. Elected as 'The Member for the Working Class', Keir Hardie went to Parliament in a workman's suit and a cloth cap. He campaigned on unemployment and other national issues, but neglected local matters, which cost him his seat at the 1895 election. He later went on to represent Merthyr Tydfil and became the first chairman of the Parliamentary Labour Party.

146. Will Thorne (1887-1946) and Jack Jones (1873-1941) were the towering giants of West Ham politics for half a century. Will Thorne (on the left of the photograph) came from Birmingham to London in search of work and found employment as a gas stoker at Beckton Gasworks. Eleanor Marx (daughter of Karl) taught him to read and write and he joined the Social Democratic Federation. In 1889 Thorne founded the Gas Workers' and General Labourers' Union which pioneered improvements in the conditions of unskilled day-labourers. He was elected to West Ham council in 1891; he also served as alderman, mayor, and in 1906 was elected as M.P. for West Ham South, later moving to the Plaistow constituency for which he sat until 1945. President of the T.U.C. in 1912, he also visited Russia in 1917. His union is now the G.M.B., one of the biggest in the country. Jack Jones (on the right) was born in Ireland and was General Organiser of Thorne's union, and, like Thorne, was also a West Ham councillor (1904-20), alderman and mayor, and served as M.P. for Silvertown from 1918-40.

147. A convoy through Stratford during the General Strike, 1926. In Stratford the General Strike coincided with a period of very high unemployment and government interference in West Ham local government, so it was well supported.

148. Crowds amassed in Stratford High Street during the General Strike, 1926. During the Strike, there were no national newspapers and the then infant B.B.C. was the only reliable source of news. Here crowds wait outside the Stratford Wireless Company shop for the next news bulletin.

149. Daisy Parsons (1890-1957) presenting prizes at Ashburton School, Custom House. The first woman mayor of West Ham, Daisy was a formidable character who was a councillor for 30 years. She had been arrested as a suffragette in 1914, drove the first trolley bus through West Ham in 1937, and was awarded the M.B.E. in 1951.

War and Disaster

In a densely populated suburb such as Stratford and West Ham, with heavy manufacturing industry and poor living conditions, tragedy and disaster are never far away, and the area has certainly suffered its fair share of calamities. One of the worst was the Silvertown Explosion, which occurred on 19 January 1917. Over 50 tonnes of T.N.T. blew up at Brunner Mond's alkali works, which had been hastily converted to manufacture the explosive as part of the war effort. 69 died in the explosion, which was heard from the Channel to the Wash, and probably remains the largest explosion ever to have occurred in Britain. The destruction to surrounding buildings and homes was enormous, and the relief effort had to be carried out amongst a population already suffering war rationing and general deprivation.

The two world wars took their toll. One hundred thousand men from West Ham served in the forces during the First World War, and the memorials to those not returning are scattered about the borough: in Lyle Park, West Silvertown; outside St Mark's church, Silvertown; in the grounds of the former West Ham bus garage; at West Ham Central Mission Baptist church. There was some local damage from bombing in the First World War, but the true horror of mass-destruction of civilian areas came with the Blitz a generation later.

In West Ham 422 service men and women died on active service during the Second World War, and 1,207 civilians were killed in the bombing raids. The Blitz of 1940 was the most destructive period in West Ham's history and heavy industry and the docks were a particular target for the bombers. The firestorm of 'Black Saturday' (7 September 1940) will never be forgotten by those who lived through it, though fortunately a considerable proportion of the population had been evacuated. The worst disaster was at South Hallsville School, where 73 people waiting for evacuation were killed when the school received a direct hit. The authorities compiled careful statistics of the number and types of air raid, the casualties and destruction, but even then the chillingly cold figures failed in the face of the sheer scale of bombing; the number of incendiary bombs hitting the borough was simply listed as 'many thousands'. Towards the end of the war the new horror of the flying bombs—the V1 and V2—brought further death and destruction, although by then the outcome of the conflict was no longer in doubt.

As a result of the war, some 14,000 houses, that is to say a quarter of all those in the borough, were destroyed by bombing. Many of the slums in Canning Town and Tidal Basin were swept away, enabling the authorities to plan a comprehensive redevelopment of the area. Road names in the new 'Keir Hardie' estate commemorate West Ham civil defence personnel killed on duty.

One of the worst peace-time tragedies occurred in 1898 when H.M.S. *Albion* was launched from Thames Ironworks. A crowd of 20,000 people gathered at the shipyard to watch the spectacle, but 38 viewing too close to the water's edge were drowned in the giant backwash as the ship slid into the Thames.

150. The Silvertown explosion, 19 January 1917, occurred at Brunner Mond & Co., a chemical plant converted to refine T.N.T. The highly dangerous process involved repeatedly melting crude explosive and dissolving the molten chemical in warm alcohol. Fifty tons of T.N.T. at the plant blew up, and in the crowded suburb of Silvertown the damage was enormous; 73 people died and over 300 were injured. The fire station, seen in this photograph, stood opposite the plant and took the full force of the blast. The sound of the explosion was heard in Norfolk and Sussex. The geographical isolation of Silvertown and strict wartime censorship both hampered the rescue work.

151. After the Silvertown explosion disaster, hundreds of people were left homeless, their properties destroyed in the blast. An Emergency Committee was set up to provide food, clothing, money and shelter while homes were repaired, relief being distributed mainly from the local churches. This photograph shows the Rev. Mr. Duthie (far right) supervising the distribution of relief at the Barking Road Wesleyan Methodist church.

152. Peace tea, June 1919, in New Providence Street (now demolished), was one of many held in the area to celebrate the Versailles peace treaty. West Ham's official war memorial took the form of a new out-patients department at Queen Mary's Hospital (also now demolished) in West Ham Lane, built by public subscription and opened in 1924.

153. Bomb damage in Cundy Road, Custom House, 1940. The street was hit on 6 September 1940, the day before 'Black Saturday' which marked the real start of the Blitz. Over 1,200 died in air raids in West Ham; one of the worst disasters occurred at South Hallsville School, where hundreds had gathered to await evacuation. The school received a direct hit, wiping out many families; 73 died in the tragedy.

154. The Silvertown Rubber Factory, hit during 'Black Saturday' (7 September 1940). The industrial areas around the docks received particular and repeated attention from the Luftwaffe.

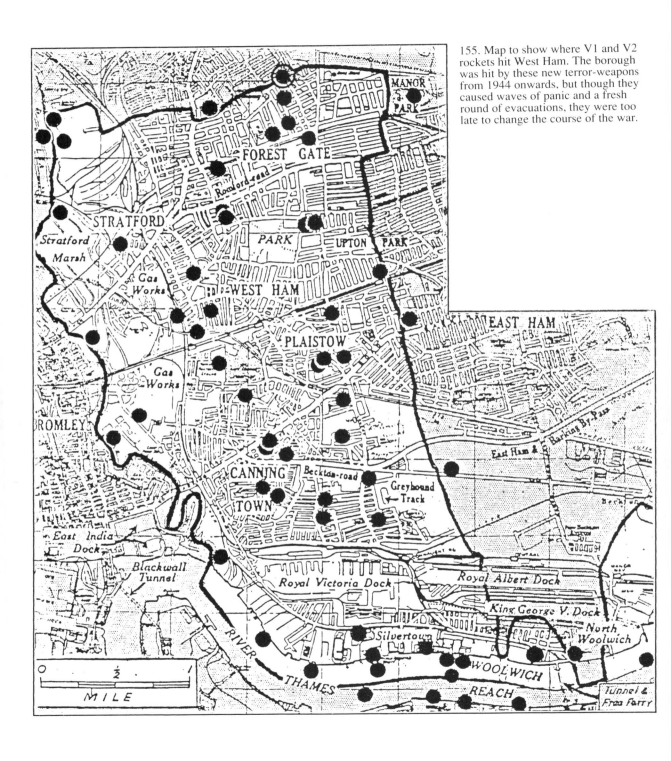

155. Map to show where V1 and V2 rockets hit West Ham. The borough was hit by these new terror-weapons from 1944 onwards, but though they caused waves of panic and a fresh round of evacuations, they were too late to change the course of the war.